LEGACY

OF

Faith

GENERATIONAL STORIES WE WILL TELL

LEGACY
OF
Faith

GENERATIONAL STORIES WE WILL TELL

HELEN JOHNSON,
DR. JULIA STANLEY-MACK,
& FAMILY

XULON PRESS

Xulon Press
2301 Lucien Way #415
Maitland, FL 32751
407.339.4217
www.xulonpress.com

Unless otherwise indicated, Scripture quotations taken from the King James Version (KJV) – *public domain.*

Printed in the United States of America

Paperback ISBN-13: 978-1-66283-728-9
Hard Cover ISBN-13: 978-1-66283-729-6
Ebook ISBN-13: 978-1-66283-730-2

Table of Contents

Introduction

<hr>

> *"...I will speak using stories of secret things from long ago. We have heard them and known them by what our ancestors have told us. WE WILL NOT KEEP THEM FROM OUR CHILDREN: We will tell those who come after about the praises of the Lord. We will tell about His power and the miracles He has done"* (Ps. 78:1–4 NCV, emphasis mine).

Julia Stanley-Mack and Helen Anderson Johnson, sisters and daughters of the Reverend Joel Allen Norris, a Church of God minister, grew up in a home where faith was talked about on a daily basis. Often, they heard stories told of answered prayers; other times, stories were told about their great grandfathers and grandparents' healings and victories. During family devotions around the kitchen table, stories of God's power were told. Many times, Reverend Joel's children were asked to sit on the floor with their Bibles for a game of Scripture Scramble while he prepared his sermons. During this competitive game, he would call out scriptures, and the children would hasten to find the scriptures. It was an intense rivalry at its best to see who could be first in finding and reading the **Word**! This was his clever way of teaching his children to love the **Word** and the wonderful stories found in the **Word**!

"Faith comes by hearing and hearing by the Word" (Rom. 10:17).

With the passing of their parents and grandparents, Julia and Helen were concerned that their children and grandchildren would not hear the wonderful stories that gripped their hearts and gave them joy in recounting them to their friends, relatives, and family. The blessings they received growing up in a home of faith shaped them into the women they are today. But what would happen to the future generations as the storytellers went to be with the Lord? How would their children know all that God had done for their family if these stories were not written down? Julia and Helen knew these stories were their faith heritage and must be **remembered.**

Legacy of Faith is the intentional and instructional project of two women to preserve the generational stories from their family history. These stories are written to encourage, strengthen, and demonstrate that the power of God is relevant today and the **Word is true!**

It is their prayer that every reader who opens this book will find these personal stories of trials by fire, pain, and sorrow and see victory and blessings that come from a God who is faithful to keep His **Word!**

Foreword

I have had the privilege of knowing Helen Johnson since my time at Lee College, now Lee University, in 1961 and 1962, where we both sang in the touring choir. Having grown up in Naples, Florida, "just down the road" from her husband Brian, I was honored to be asked to be a part of their wedding. After I left Lee and joined the Army a couple of years later, our paths parted for most of our working years. However, our paths converged again in Cleveland, Tennessee, when I retired from Price Waterhouse (now PricewaterhouseCoopers) in 1996 and moved to Cleveland, to which they had moved in 1989. My deceased wife and current wife and I have enjoyed many visits with them in their home, at restaurants, on trips, and so on. I have heard many of the stories in this book over the years and have seen much of her legacy of faith in action. She is part of an amazing family with remarkable examples of life experiences, which demonstrate incredible faith in many different situations.

o *Legacy of Faith* brings an incredible variety of real-life examples of people living out faith in action. As you read these stories, you will find an astonishing variety of people, including:

o Her father and uncle, historic figures in the Church of God;

o Julia Lee, the mother of Joel and Marshall Norris, claimed to be related to Robert E. Lee;

o Linh, Helen's niece born in Vietnam, who, at age ten, escaped with her thirteen-year-old sister from the North Vietnamese army on a small refugee boat to Thailand, where she caught a US plane transporting Amerasian orphans to the US; and

o Al Capon!

Your faith will be reinforced by the faith in action revealed in this book. I highly recommend it.

Grady M. Townsend

Grady M. Townsend

Cleveland, Tennessee

Former Partner, Price Waterhouse

Acknowledgments

B rian Johnson, my husband of fifty-eight years, whose love, patience, and guidance have inspired me and whose excellent typing skills have blessed me throughout this project.

Dr. Jason Robinson, and his example as a godly professor, caring teacher, and for his support at the onset of the project.

Cindi Morrow, whose faith and friendship over the years have been a true inspiration.

Grady and Dede Townsend, for their longtime friendship, encouragement, and technical support.

Ronald Norris, for his long hours of research and willingness to share the history of the Norris family.

Janell Cobb Kennedy, for sharing the historical facts of the Cobb family.

Dr. Keith Cobb, for his support and willingness to share the tragedy of Mama Cobb.

Marshall, Trey, and Chad Norris, for sharing their stories of faith and history of the M. B. Norris family.

Sharon Aspinwall

Linh Hopkins

Minh Aimone

Eric Johnson

Tyler Johnson

Gloria Adams

Philip Norris

Kevin Townsend

For all those who willingly shared their memories and personal family pictures for the book.

To the God who has given us the legacy of faith!

Dedication

We are commanded to recount the generational blessings God promised to Abraham that his seeds would be like the sand of the seashore and as many as the stars in the sky. This is our commanded blessing through Jesus Christ for our children and grandchildren. They must know their legacy, and **we must tell!**

"Blessed are the dead, who die in the Lord from henceforth ...that they may rest from their labors; and their works do follow them" **(Rev. 14:13).**

The stories of Joel A. Norris, M. B. Norris, and Foye Norris, sons of Allen Preston Norris, who had a twin brother named John Wesley Norris, were all ministers of the gospel and lived a life of faith so their children and grandchildren would know their blessed heritage and incredible inheritance left to them because of God's faithfulness. They loved the **Word**, lived the **Word**, and preached the **Word**. They left to us the responsibility of passing on these testimonials of faith that **we must tell!**

Allen Preston Norris

This book is dedicated to the generations of godly men and women in our families who have gone before us but whose faith stories of miracles, healings, and deliverance have been passed on to us, and **we must tell!** These stories have shaped our lives and established principles based on biblical truths that our children must know.

This book is also dedicated to our children, grandchildren, great grandchildren, and those not yet born. They are generational stories that **we must tell!**

The Cobb Family

Beatrice Cobb

Written by: Helen Johnson, daughter of Beatrice, with help from her first cousin, Keith Cobb.

*B*eatrice Cobb, our mother, was the first child born to Omer and Inez Cobb. They lived in Glennville, Georgia. She was a gifted musician and served as a pastor's wife for many years. She raised eight children, Haven, Helen, Gerald, Joel Allen Jr., Julia, Ronnie, Gloria, and Philip.

Beatrice Cobb Norris

Marjorie Beatrice Cobb was born on November 22, 1922, and the first child of Omer Watson Cobb and Inez DeLoach Cobb of Glennville, Georgia, located in Tattnall County. There were eight children in Mother's family. My granddaddy Cobb operated a grocery store on Barnard Street in downtown Glennville. He also opened a neighborhood store in his home. Their beautiful home in town had a wraparound porch, so he enclosed a section of the porch for a store, where he stocked staples and other essential goods that his neighbors in the community could purchase. My grandmother operated the home store while managing the house chores and children. He later started a rolling store out of his truck that serviced rural areas of the county. He and my grandmother supplied milk from their cows and delivered milk and butter to the neighbors. Early in the morning, before going to school, my mother would deliver quarts of fresh milk to the front doorsteps of their neighbors. Years later, Mother told me that the proceeds from the milk sales helped pay for her piano lessons.

Their home was located across the street from the Glennville Church of God, where my grandfather was an active member serving as a church clerk and working in the Sunday school ministry. He was influential in building and establishing the Church of God in Glennville. He and the Reverend M. B. Norris, from Jesup, Georgia, who planted many new churches for the denomination in southeast Georgia, went to merchants in Glennville and raised funds to build the church.

He always encouraged children to attend church, bringing packages of chewing gum and candy to the ones who attended Sunday school. He would also give pennies to children who had birthdays, one for each year of their age for the child to drop in the offering plate. "Happy Birthday" was sung following the birthday offering. As a result of his love and faithfulness to the children's ministry, his own children, grandchildren, and great grandchildren are in ministry today.

"Suffer little children and forbid them not, to come unto me: for of such is the kingdom of heaven" (Matt. 19:14).

Education was always a priority in my mother's family. My great-aunt, Inez, Papa Cobb's sister, was my first-grade teacher and also served as principal of the elementary school I attended in Glennville. As a result of hard work, wise choices, and strong, unwavering, uncompromising Christian faith in God, there are teachers, pastors, youth pastors, ministers' wives, coaches, bankers, doctors—grandson, Dr. Keith Cobb, and great-grandson, Dr. Blake Norman—and other members of his family serving in the medical field. His example to his family, his dedication to God, his prayers for his family, and his giving all set in order blessings for his children and grandchildren, and their lives are making a difference in today's world. The seeds Papa Cobb planted in us during those early years are still bearing fruit. His faithfulness to God, the Bible, and the Word created a legacy and commanded blessing for those in his family, and we **must tell of the marvelous acts of God!** Only eternity will reveal the entire scope of influence one's home can have when it is Christ-centered, filled with God's love, and dedicated to the service of others.

"And their seeds shall be known among the Gentiles, and their offspring among the people: all that see them shall acknowledge them that they are the seed, which the Lord has blessed" (Isa. 6:19).

Inez DeLoach Cobb

The saying, "Behind every successful man is a great woman," is certainly true when describing my grandmother, Inez DeLoach Cobb. She was strong and courageous. She was an incredible cook and immaculate housekeeper. No one in the family today can duplicate her fresh-creamed corn recipe, cornbread dressing, peach cobbler, and pot roast. **Believe me, I have tried.**

My Grandmother Inez "Mama Cobb" was the quintessential Southern lady!

Another outstanding talent of Inez "Mama Cobb," as she was affectionately called, was her creative sewing ability. She operated the store at home while taking care of her children and grandchildren's needs. During the mid-1850s, print material, known as feed sacks, were used instead of paper or plastic bags to transport flour. Because many people repurposed everything they could, the feed sacks often contained fashionable prints so they could be used for the purpose of making garments. Mama Cobb would ask her children and grandchildren to pick out a feed sack from her supply in the store, and then she would take the fabric we selected and make beautiful girls' dresses adorned with eyelet trim and exquisite bows. When she would ask me to pick out a feed sack so she could make one of her "designer" dresses, I felt so special, just like a princess! Later, when we moved to Arkansas, where Daddy pastored, I would eagerly await the mail to be delivered to receive the creation(s) she had made for me.

I remember my Aunt Cathryn telling me how Mama Cobb made dresses for her and the other daughters while they were in college ...those dresses and garments were beautifully made out of a heart full of love.

She is still an incredible inspiration to her family. Her love for her children and grandchildren was always on display. Proverbs 31:25–28 describes Mama Cobb perfectly:

Mama Cobb and Her Children

"Strength and honor are her clothing; and she shall rejoice in time to come, she openeth her mouth with wisdom; and in her tongue is the law of kindness, she looketh well to the ways of her household, and

eateth not the bread of idleness, her children arise up and call her blessed; her husband also, and he praiseth her."

Things weren't always easy for Mama Cobb, though. When she was just twenty-four, she encountered grief, as no mother should ever have to endure. Her first son, Howell, just a two-year-old toddler at the time, was trapped inside a burning building. "Mama Cobb" charged into the building and found him burning and crying. "I recall the dreadful sight and smell of my mother emerging from the burning building carrying my brother in her arms." Beatrice told Dr. Keith during her interview. Although both Mama Cobb and Howell were promptly taken to the hospital, Howell died of smoke inhalation.

Beatrice Cobb Norris and Her Siblings

My nephew, Dr. Keith Cobb, who practices medicine in Richmond Hill, Georgia, and who is the son of Don Cobb (the youngest of Omer and Inez "Mama Cobb"), wrote a book on grief, and in his book, *The Grief Survival Handbook: A Guide from Heartache to Healing,* he speaks of the tragic event.

Howell's funeral was held the day before Christmas Eve in 1924. "Inez had already purchased presents for her three children, including

Howell. She later quietly opened his presents and placed them in a trunk, never to be played with by her son."

Dr. Cobb asked his grandmother, decades later, how she overcame such a devastating loss. "I never have" was her response (Cobb 2010).

"Though I walk in the midst of trouble, you will revive me, and your right hand will save" (**Ps. 138:7–8**).

M. B. Norris, Minister, Church Planter, and State Overseer

The Norris Family

Marshall Norris

*M*arshall Norris is the grandson of M. B. and Jewel Norris. He is married to Laurie Norris, and they have three children, Jillian and twin brothers Chad and Trey. He works in the insurance industry in his own business. They live in Jesup, Georgia.

"Granddaddy, is something wrong?"

This was not an ordinary question from a little boy who loved his grandfather more than he could truly begin to understand at the tender age of eight. He was outside in the yard when I walked up to him, saw the look on his face, and realized something was definitely not right.

"Granddaddy, you look sad today; is everything okay?"

His voice was emotionally charged, and like those occasions when the sun is shining but raining at the same time, I saw tears, and then a smile began to form as he delivered a completely unexpected response, "Today is the day I lost my boys . . ."

Time tends to erase much of our bad memories while human nature embellishes the good times. Mysteriously, it seems that God blessed me with an ability to recall a whole lot of the good and just enough of the bad to remind us all that God is the One who takes us from the mountaintop to the valley and back again.

Marshall Blanco Norris, also known as "M. B. Norris," was born on February 12, 1900, and his father, Allen Preston Norris, was a Baptist pastor in a farming region of Southwest Georgia, not far from Dothan, Alabama. His mother was Julia Lee, with roots in Virginia, and proud to claim relation to Robert E. Lee.

The Norris Brothers

M. B.'s siblings included Milton, Joel, Sam, John (J. P.), Harrison, Foye, May, Minnie, Salie, Florence, Jessie, and Lena Bell. His father's twin brother, John Wesley Norris, was a Baptist minister in that area also.

M. B. was a healthy son who dropped out of school very early to help his family financially. He married his sweetheart Jewell Williams Norris on her sixteenth birthday when he was just twenty-one years old himself, and they never separated for nearly sixty years of marriage.

During the 1920s, even though M. B. was raised in a Christian home, he lived life on his own moral terms. He worked hard and had natural leadership abilities, but with little to no formal education, he had never learned to read. Therefore, utilizing his God-given talents, he pursued roles that allowed his personality to shine.

One such job involved ice delivery to homes in the Miami Beach area, and one of his patrons in the late 1920s was a notorious figure named Al Capone. I did not hear this story firsthand, but my father shared how his dad was one of the few men allowed to enter the Capone mansion, where men stood in doorways with Tommy guns and locked the place down like a fortress. The most intriguing aspect of the story is that M. B. developed a casual rapport with Capone around the pool table on those days he delivered ice.

I have often wondered what it must have been like to be invited into Al Capone's sanctuary, what they may have talked about, and if M. B. allowed Capone to beat him at pool just to play it safe! When I was fourteen years old, my dad bought a second-hand pool table from a neighbor. Dad and I played pool every night that first week or two when one afternoon, after school, I heard a knock on the door. Upon opening the door, I saw Granddaddy smiling ear to ear as he stated, "I heard you have a pool table!"

I answered yes and asked if he would like to play a game. Of course, he nodded yes, and as I set the balls up for break, all while figuring I should take it easy on him, I asked if he would like to go first in a game of eight-ball. Once again, the smile and nod were affirmative.

As I watched with an unknowingly misplaced smile on my face, Granddaddy addressed the table and began taking aim. The main thing I noticed was that his hands were shaking as he prepared to shoot, but moments before the strike, the hands froze completely still. He broke the rack, and all the balls scattered furiously. I do not remember how many balls went in a pocket, but at least one did because his turn continued. With each shot, his hands would shake, then freeze, only to strike with perfect precision until every one of the balls were off the table, including the "fata accompli" eight-ball. I was amazed that at seventy-four, Granddaddy had beaten me without my ever enjoying a turn.

I quickly asked if he would like to play again, but he just smiled and declined the invitation ...we never played again. I figure M. B. Norris won his fair share with Capone, or the man would not have enjoyed playing against him. But I still believed he let Capone win a few just to keep it interesting.

Sometime around 1930, spending way too much time hustling in pool halls while also playing farm league baseball as a pitcher who possessed an unusual ability to throw with either hand, he began showing clear signs of alcoholism. Heartbreakingly, his brother Sam died from cirrhosis of the liver at the age of twenty-seven, and Sam's untimely death nearly destroyed M. B., as they were very close. Thankfully, there were people in his life that shared God's love and reminded him of his Christian upbringing ...What could he do but call on God?

Eventually, M. B. gained employment with the Florida Power and Light Company, where he was constantly asked to accept management responsibilities. He would decline such opportunities due to his well-kept secret of being unable to read. But eventually, he did accept roles where he could take reports home, and his wife would read for him and complete his paperwork. He also attempted to live for Christ, but the old life kept calling him back.

Sensing a call on his life to preach, he began to seek God's direction in becoming a fifth-generation Norris to act upon God's call to ministry; however, by then, he was doing very well financially employed with the power company. Even as the Great Depression was in full swing, he owned a nice home and was blessed to provide for five children (Ella-V, William, Marshall Jr., Harry, and Elaine). Therefore, when he approached Jewell with the idea of following God's leading into the ministry, she was fearful and resisted, saying, "We have been blessed; how could God ask us to give so much up at a time like this?" This stalemate lasted for months until that sad day when tragedy struck their precious family.

It was a bright Saturday morning, and Ella-V reminded her daddy that he had promised to take her brothers to get their hairs cut. She was the oldest child and truly enjoyed the big sister role. So, M. B. took his sons to the barber. I don't know how far the barbershop was from home, but as they returned ...walking through the neighborhoods on a beautiful day ...the unimaginable happened.

Looking down the street, M. B. could see a truck erratically progressing toward them. Even though William was the oldest, he was sick that day, and M. B. held his hand as they walked. The two younger boys, Little Marshall and Harry, were not many steps ahead as they playfully made their way home. M. B.'s sense of danger quickened, and he instructed the boys away from the road and into a yard. Even though they followed their father's instructions, the truck was on them in an instant. M. B. could clearly see the driver now, as he drunkenly laughed and appeared to intentionally veer off the road to chase them down in the yard. The sound of both boys being hit by the truck could not be heard, just felt. M. B. immediately swept his sons into his arms, one already dead and the other may as well have been.

How could anything good come out of something so horribly devastating? In 1987, my grandfather was eighty-seven years old and running a revival in Columbus, Georgia. A local radio station was interviewing this man that lost his sons to an act that could only be described as pure evil. Yet fifty-five years later, he was smiling and genuinely exhibited so much love that the interviewer could not believe the testimony he was hearing. M. B. shared that for nearly a year after the tragedy, all he could do was cry. Through continuous tears of anguish and misery, every day, he asked God, *"Why did You kill my sons?"*

Stepping back into the story, it was the early 1930s, and Jewell now believed that God truly had called her husband to the ministry, but M. B. was undone, with no direction or hope. In due course, after months of questions that could more accurately be described as accusations, God answered, and M. B. was listening. The Lord spoke and said, "I didn't kill your sons. The *evil* in that man killed your sons!"

After so many tears and so much loss, M. B. chose hope over despair; a hope that he would see Little Marshall and Harry again one day in heaven. His heart finally melted, and he was truly a changed man. From that day forward, M. B. was free from despair, and people who met him never felt judged; only unconditional love came from his brilliant blue eyes. Therefore, people responded to the hope he so freely shared with anyone willing to sit for a while and talk about their troubles.

Some would ask, how do you know that God changed M. B. Norris? The answer is also amazing. At the height of the Great Depression, M. B. resigned from his job and moved his family to Southeast Georgia, where he immediately entered the ministry. God gave him a passion for planting churches, and the Holy Ghost delivered the necessary spiritual knowledge. He would build brush arbors where necessary, hold tent meetings when he could, and God changed the brokenhearted through M. B.'s ministry. However, he still could not read, so Jewell read the Bible to him, and he would memorize the verses so that he could deliver the sermons. As time passed, M. B. asked God to teach him to read, and I have heard him testify that God taught him to read miraculously *overnight*. But the real proof of a truly changed and reborn man came when God began to plant forgiveness in his heart for the man that killed his sons!

The drunken man that struck down M. B. Norris's sons was a wealthy businessman in the Miami area. Apparently, he also had trouble with alcohol, and based on overwhelming evidence, was sentenced to life in prison. He was also ordered to make restitution to my grandfather by deeding over an empty lot used for parking in downtown Miami, right across from the courthouse, and a residentially zoned lot on Miami Beach.

After a year or two, M. B. wrote a letter to the prison warden and asked if he could visit the man in prison. The warden was very cautious but agreed to speak with M. B. about the possibility. Who knows what was discussed or how M. B. convinced him of his sincerity, but eventually, he was allowed to meet with the man over several days in a series of short sessions.

Can we imagine, for a moment, what the murderer must have thought when told that the father of the children he killed while drunk wanted to visit with him? I have heard my grandfather's testimony about these events. He said God caused him to understand the Scriptures regarding forgiveness, such as, "if you forgive others who sin against you, your heavenly Father will forgive you." M. B. forgave the man face to face but also shared that God had forgiveness waiting for him, too, through the blood of Christ. The man had never met anyone that demonstrated such love and compassion, and before leaving the prison, my grandfather led the man to his Lord and Savior through a sinner's prayer of repentance.

But the testimony did not stop there; the man had a family with children of his own, and through the compassion that God placed in his heart, M. B. wrote a letter to the governor of Florida, asking that he be pardoned. As I understand, the guilty man was eventually released to return to his family. Surely, he was changed forever, and my grandparents, along with their two little boys, are enjoying eternity with the man that devastated their lives. What Satan meant for evil, God turned to good!

By 1965, M. B. had relocated to Bainbridge after transferring from a very successful period as pastor at a church called Piney Grove, just outside Odum, Georgia. At the church in Bainbridge, God blessed again, and the church had grown significantly. One Sunday nearing his sixty-fifth birthday, a state overseer visited the church, and afterward, they talked "shop" for a while. During the conversation, the overseer mentioned something about M. B.'s soon retirement, and he responded with a big grin, saying that he was truly enjoying God's work and did not expect to be retiring any time soon ...particularly with the way the Holy Ghost was moving amongst the congregation.

Not long after, his wife suffered a massive stroke that paralyzed her entire right side, and while attempting to care for her needs, M. B.'s health had slipped to the point he was in the hospital. Actually, his health had deteriorated to the stage that doctors suggested the family should prepare for his homegoing.

As he would testify later, M. B. had been praying all night and day in his hospital bed when God spoke to him with a question, "Did I call you to preach, or did man?"

His response was, "You did, Lord!"

Then God said, "Preach My Word!"

M. B.'s response was, "But Lord, I am sick and dying. I need Your healing touch if I am to leave this place."

The answer to prayer, just like the overnight gift of reading and so many other miraculous events in his life, came immediately. M. B. was released from the hospital just a day or two later with complete health, and the best part is that he worked full-time for the Lord, traveling and preaching on a full schedule until God called him home many years later.

In the mid-1980s, the Church of God was in deep debate about the membership rules of the denomination. Those holiness-based rules had been in place long before M. B. joined the Church of God in the early 1930s. I was already married and living outside of Georgia, but a close friend and longtime pastor shared this story with me not long after it took place.

At the time, the state of Georgia was already separated into North and South Georgia for administrative purposes, and the South Georgia Camp Meeting in Tifton was in a large building that Granddaddy called a tabernacle. It looked like a large church, but it was open on the sides during services and meetings.

As a child from the age of six to sixteen, I traveled with Granddaddy every summer to revivals all over the Southeast, including camp meetings in Doraville and Tifton, Georgia. At a young age, I was bored during the business portion of those meetings; however, I knew their importance, as the attendees were always focused on seeking God's direction for the denomination.

According to that friend and a memory that is surely not as sharp as it was thirty years ago, M. B. Norris stood up in one of those business meetings in Tifton and began to speak. He shared that he had been praying all day and night for several days leading up to Camp Meeting (a reoccurring theme with him). He went on to share that his convictions had not changed regarding the commitments he made to follow the membership rules of the denomination when he joined the church as a young man. He said, "I live by those rules, and always will, but I do not believe we can place our convictions on others today."

Just a few months later, the recording of M. B.'s unrehearsed address to the ministers attending that South Georgia business meeting was played before a business meeting at the General Assembly ...and out of that session, the church voted to change the membership rules, renaming them "Guidelines to Live By." They are best understood as the Doctrinal Commitments of the Church of God today.

There are so many stories that could be shared about my grandfather, enough to write a book instead of just a short story.

One of those stories involved Finis Jennings Dake, of the acclaimed Dake Annotated Reference Bible, who spent the better part of a summer at their house each evening, asking M. B. Norris questions about Bible interpretation. Granddaddy had a copy of that Bible when I was growing up, but I did not know the connection between Dake and my grandfather until my dad shared the story behind the story.

Dake and my grandfather were roughly the same age, but there was a world of difference between the two men. Dake was flamboyant and had spent time in prison, but was also known for memorizing thousands of scriptures and compiling copious notes in the margins of his personal reference Bible. M. B. Norris, on the other hand, was known for his genuine humility, gentleness, and love for everyone he met, and many sought out his insight of God's Word, which could have only been imparted by the Holy Ghost.

Interestingly, my grandfather was known for designing and utilizing large hand-painted canvas charts used to deliver sermons explaining Revelation and end-time prophecy. To have so little formal education and no seminary degree behind his name, M. B. Norris had a deep understanding and love for the intricacies of the book of Revelation. He also enjoyed a rare ability to teach, preach, and lead people into a deeper understanding of the complete Word of God. Rarely do we hear ministers today teach on "types and antitypes," where the New Testament is enfolded in the Old, and the Old Testament unfolded in the New. For example, in teaching Revelation, he knew it required edification from the book of Daniel to fully explain God's prophetic message.

As we know, some men are called to shepherd a flock of a local church, some are called to missions, and some are called to evangelize. My grandfather was a church planter. Over and over again, he would announce a revival in a town where no Church of God existed, set up a brush arbor or tent, begin a revival that could last for weeks at a time, and organize a church with new members who had just given their hearts to the Lord. Hopefully, someone would donate a small piece of property or the money to purchase it, and others would donate their time to physically build and equip the church. At that point, M. B. would sometimes become the pastor for a short time or place someone else in the role. This happened in many, many small towns from Georgia to Arkansas and all points in between.

Jewel and Marshall in Later Life

Not long before my grandmother Jewell died in 1980, the three of us were together at their old farmhouse outside Odum. That morning, I remember my grandmother being so excited to share a dream with her husband. It had been roughly fifty years since they lost their sons in that terrible event, but she had seen them vividly in her dream. They were waving to her on the other side of a river. She said the place was beautiful, and she could hear them calling for her to come on over; they were waiting for her. The two of them cried and talked about how they hoped for God's soon return, and they prayed they both would cross that river together to be with Jesus and hold their sons once again. I just watched and listened as they held each other and cried.

At the age of eighty-seven, my grandfather had driven by himself to Columbus and truly enjoyed a successful revival, which lasted all week. He had been interviewed on the radio and shared his story one more time to a man that was truly amazed. I know this because the interview was recorded, and we can still listen to their voices today. However, the morning after driving the 200-mile journey home to his farm in Odum, Georgia, he had a stroke. My father found him sitting in his chair, tapping a cane on the floor, and saying, "No, no, no." Granddaddy sometimes called Satan "Beelzebub," and I believe he was probably speaking back to the devil, knowing that his God was more powerful than any weapon the devil would try to use. He knew how to fight the good fight of faith and call upon God in times of trouble, similarly to when God healed him of a burst appendicitis during his early ministry and a heart attack after investing four years in Arkansas as Church of God state overseer, and then again after he retired from active ministry and was dying in a hospital bed. Although he was scheduled to preach a revival the upcoming week at a church where his brother Joel's daughter, Dr. Julie Stanley-Mack, pastored, it was finally his time to see Jesus face to face, hold his sons again, reunite with his sweetheart Jewell, and receive his eternal reward.

As life moved forward swiftly, my summers with Granddaddy became echoes of distant memories. That fall in 1987, I received word about

Granddad's stroke, and I remember running through the Atlanta airport to get back to my car. Thankfully, I arrived at Wayne Memorial Hospital in time to see him before he passed. He was unconscious, but I was close now and whispered into his ear, saying, "Granddaddy, it's Marshall. If you know me, squeeze my hand," and he did! Our bond was special; I carried his name (another Little Marshall) and spent so much of my formative years traveling with him during those treasured summers. It was almost as if I enjoyed two fathers in my life. My granddad was the gentle and saintly influence that guided me into my adult life while my father, a self-proclaimed preacher's kid, modeled a zest for life outdoors, sports, family, and faith that has always reminded me of where I came from.

My father, David Thaddeus Norris, was the sixth child born to M. B. and Jewell Norris in February 1939. He and his younger brother, Eddie, were the gifts given to them after the death of their sons, Marshall Jr. and Harry. Sadly, representing the last of his siblings, Dad passed into eternity a few short months ago, in December 2020.

My parents, David and Kara Bowen Norris, were married in 1960, and they, too, were never separated for sixty years. Kara blessed her children as a stay-at-home mom and later became an exceptional floral designer. She was in her mid-thirties before discovering she had a beautiful voice and began singing in the choir and at weddings when asked, which is miraculous because she was completely deaf in one ear and wore a hearing aid in the other.

Dad was an accomplished man with multiple degrees in education and administration that propelled him from beloved coach and teacher to principal, and before retiring, the road culminated in his being elected as the Wayne County school superintendent. Several generations of children and parents of all races loved, adored, and respected my father as someone who truly cared enough to do more than say the right things; he did the right things.

In the late 1960s and early 1970s, the local school system moved toward integration, and a few children from the Black community took the first early steps before desegregation was fully initiated. Dad was a football coach when one brave young man enrolled and decided to try out for the team. I remember the times and the first children to integrate early into my third-grade class, but I never heard my father talk about the story I am about to share.

Several years ago, while reading the local newspaper published in Jesup, Georgia, my eyes widened as an article about the first African American to integrate the Wayne County school system mentioned my father by name. Recognizing the events of that time, the person interviewed shared stories of discrimination, but he mostly focused on one individual that made all the difference in his life, a man he called Coach Norris.

One story he shared was about Coach Norris personally protecting him from harm in the locker room, and later, how my father provided him with a real opportunity to engage and win the respect of his new team and classmates. The next year, when desegregation was mandated, it appeared the things my father did to help the one were perhaps instrumental in helping the many become assimilated much easier than some had anticipated in that newly integrated environment.

I have often wondered what made my father different than most, someone that would stand up for the disadvantaged or minority where others may say the right things but not act upon them. Dad was always a friend to everyone, particularly those willing to work hard and play by the rules. He was a respected leader who did not shy from discipline but was very much loved by those that benefited from his caring and supportive hand.

Just shortly before the 2020 covid pandemic, I bumped into a well-known figure in the local community. This man was born with a handicap, and while growing up, he was ridiculed by his classmates. Dad took a special interest in the kid, helped him improve his self-esteem through sports, and he graduated with a football scholarship to the University of Georgia, where he was also drafted by the NFL. The man never played professionally, as he returned home to marry his sweetheart and enjoy a successful career.

Sadly, the man had recently experienced a stroke and was just beginning to move about town again. It had been many years, but I recognized him immediately as we stood in line to purchase our BBQ plates.

As he turned and saw me, I smiled, said hello, and we shook hands. Then he looked at me, and with tears forming in this towering man's eyes, he said, "Marshall, your father is the reason I received an education, and I am the man I am today because of him!"

I teared up too because I knew exactly what he meant. My father affected people, he helped people at the point of their needs, and he made a difference in their lives when they needed help the most ...just like his father, M. B. Norris!

As a son who believed in miracles, my father experienced many such events in his life, but there were four definitive miracles over the course of forty years that immediately come to mind, three that involved physicians informing us to prepare for the end. Thankfully, God had other plans, and Dad loved to testify!

The first event happened when Dad returned to the Lord after running in the opposite direction for so long. I am certain God never turned His back, but from a young age, Dad chose to pursue life on his own terms, and very much like his father, he did not return until his thirties.

Prior to his conversion, there was a simmering fire that could easily be ignited. David Norris was running, and he didn't want my mother to enjoy the Lord either. He would often tell her that if she went to church, not to hang around afterward and come home immediately after the preaching. Even though my mother began attending regularly and taking me, he made sure he was in the woods on Sundays. Little did we know how much God was dealing with him, and on one such Sunday, Dad would testify that God spoke to him audibly, saying, "Why are you fighting Me; why are you running?"

There was more that God said, but the main thing I remember is Dad saying he opened the door to his truck and fell to the ground, weeping and asking God for forgiveness.

Someone may ask again, "How do you know your father was a changed man?"

Well, the answer was readily apparent. Shortly thereafter, while on a hunting trip with a handful of hunting buddies and their sons, I saw firsthand the new man. After hunting all day, and now gathered on a houseboat on the Altamaha River, one of the men had learned of Dad's conversion and began teasing him. This man was drinking a certain brand of whiskey named "Lord Calvert," and he teased my father about "loving the Lord," saying, "Take a drink, David. I know you love the Lord."

In the half-lit room, I could see my father's eyes turn bloodshot and his body tense for a fight, but after a few minutes, he stood up and excused himself from the table. We never went on another hunting trip with those men, but I knew for certain this was not the man he used to be!

As mentioned, the miracles in Dad's life were numerous and could fill a book themselves. There was the time he contracted Rocky Mountain spotted fever. He was in a coma and near death for many days before they discovered the tick bite. Then, there was the time he contracted a rare condition associated with bird dust that destroyed the oxygen in his lungs (he owned pigeons). The doctors identified a mass in his lungs and sent him home to get his affairs in order, saying it was highly possible he would not survive surgery. Community churches of all denominations prayed that weekend, and when they took fresh pictures of his lungs on Monday, each picture revealed more of the mass disappearing until the last picture showed clean lungs. Who wouldn't shout hallelujah? Dad certainly loved to testify about that one!

In 2010, Dad was very unhealthy and his weight had ballooned due to water retention. After a prolonged battle with psoriatic arthritis and complications from diabetes, followed by multiple hospitalizations and rehabilitation events at a local nursing home, he appeared to be at an end once again. The doctors were saying he had lung cancer, and an allergic reaction to blue dye had caused his kidneys to completely fail, which required dialysis. After being transported from the nursing home back to the hospital in Jesup, it was learned the hospitals in Brunswick and Savannah were refusing to accept his transfer request. Apparently, those hospitals believed there was no hope! However, I suggested we try Jacksonville, and thankfully, Saint Vincent's Hospital accepted his transfer.

As the ambulance arrived around midnight, a world-renowned lung specialist, who was assigned to President George W. Bush at a G-8 conference on Sea Island a few years earlier, just happened to be in the ER that night. This doctor looked at Dad's chart and asked my mother if he could operate on him immediately. Mom answered, "Yes!"

The doctor removed one of Dad's lungs from his chest, scraped it out, and put it back in place. Later, the doctor told the family there were barnacles in his lung, like cement, and he just scraped them out. The interesting preamble to this revelation was the pictures from a few weeks earlier showing bleeding, cancerous ulcers in his lungs. God dried the cancer up, and the doctor just scraped them out! But we were not yet out of the woods . . .

Still at St. Vincent's nearly two months later, Dad was close to death's door. He had an unusually aggressive MRSA-type staph infection contracted in the hospital and had been on a ventilator for over a month. Doctors were giving up again, and I found myself praying and asking God for eight more years. I don't know why I prayed for eight, but I spent time on Dad's farm in meditation and prayer, and that is what I asked God to provide. A few days later, Dad somehow pulled the ventilator off himself in his unconscious state and walked out of the hospital through the Lord's strength just days later. He had lost one hundred pounds, no longer needed to take insulin for diabetes, and, to top it off, God brought his kidney function back to 100 percent!

The events in Jacksonville took place eleven years ago, but my father died this past Christmas, roughly ten years after I prayed that God would give us eight more with him. My brother Thad and I were with him when he departed for home, and it was one of the most emotional events I have ever experienced. At the point of his departure, I remembered the prayer for eight more years, then realized God had given us ten! How could I be upset with God? I was blessed and highly favored, and now a great cloud of witnesses encircled me!

So, the story of our family continues onward. Named for two of my grandfathers, I am Marshall Alexander Norris, the eldest of three children, born in 1961 to David and Kara Bowen Norris. I have a sister,

Camille Norris Sellers, and a younger brother, David Thad Norris Jr. To say I am blessed to be a part of the legacy of those that have gone before me is without hesitation.

My wife Laurie and I were married in 1985 after meeting at Georgia Southern University in Statesboro, Georgia. Our three children— Jillian, born in 1990, and Chad and Trey, twin sons born to us in 1995—are further proof that God intends for us to go forward, for "such a time as this."

As with many families, our journey has not been easy. Our first child, Jillian, was born to us after much prayer and petition before God and has been our little girl for almost thirty-one years now, although she is now married to Nathan Love and a mom to Eden and Henry. Our second child, Marshall Alexander Norris Jr., was born and lived among us for only a few hours, only to meet Jesus face to face before we were ready to let him go. In my lifetime, it was the most traumatic time and one that has changed me forever.

Our family has experienced grief and loss, but the story does not end there. Within one year following the death of our son, God took us from a place of despair to one of joy, as our twin sons were prophesied to be born during a revival service in Bonham, Texas. As we stood before the Lord, a Church of God pastor, Reverend Dwayne Evors, laid his hands on us and petitioned the Lord to give back a *double portion* of all that the devil had stolen from us. Almost nine months to the day, Chad Wesley and Trey Michael were born to us. And our family was complete.

Today, our daughter lives in Kansas with her family and has a flourishing career after much education and time spent abroad during her studies. Our sons, Chad and Trey, are ready to answer the call of God in their lives, as they are busy completing their education at the Pentecostal Theological Seminary in Cleveland, Tennessee. Once again, what the devil meant for our harm, God has used for His glory.

Trey and Chad Norris

It is truly amazing how God weaves the tapestry of our lives. Our paths crossed with Helen and Brian Johnson because of the decision Chad and Trey made in choosing to further their education in Cleveland, Tennessee. The blessing they have been to us has been nothing short of amazing. The family legacy we share with Helen and her family give us a bond that only grows stronger. With each and every visit and each and every hour we spend together, we are simply reminded that God had such a beautiful plan when He created the family. We are forever blessed with the Norris legacy we share and the mandate given to us to serve Him into the next generation. To God be the glory.

Trey Norris

Trey is the son of Marshall and Laurie Norris. He is also the twin brother to Chad Norris. He currently is pursuing a master's degree from the Church of God Pentecostal Theological Seminary, in Cleveland, Tennessee, and when not in school, lives in Jesup, Georgia.

When I reflect upon God, I can honestly narrow down my feelings to one, all-encompassing word—gratitude. The hardest trial of my life came for me at the age of twenty-three. It all began during spring break 2019, and I can honestly say I have not thought of God or approached Him the same way since.

I remember coming home to my parents' house for a relaxing week after a few hard weeks of study. At the time, I was going to Pentecostal Theological Seminary in Cleveland, Tennessee, pursuing what I knew was a call from God on my life. It was during that week when I started to experience very strange occurrences in my body. I remember waking in the middle of the night and experiencing a strong tingling and numbing in my hands and feet. These sensations were strong enough to wake me from a deep sleep, and I had never experienced anything remotely of the sort in my life. Upon waking the next day, I just attributed the experience to something weird that I had eaten the day before—possibly food poisoning—or something similar. I would soon find out that I was sadly mistaken.

It was after I returned to school a week later that I began to experience the symptoms more regularly. There was no perceived pattern or cause that I could put my finger on; the "episodes," for lack of a better term, would occur randomly at any time. It was also during this time that the sensations began to progress into things much more serious. Not only would my hands and feet go numb, but also random fingers and toes would start twitching uncontrollably. Whatever this thing was somehow began to attack my face or brain as well; there would be parts of my face that would twitch or stiffen, and it would be difficult for me to talk. I described the symptoms as "stroke-like" at the time; even though I had never experienced a stroke, the sensations felt like how I imagined a stroke to feel. Needless to say, I began to see doctors and specialists to determine what was going on with me.

They tested me for pretty much everything; diabetes—those tests came back negative; all sorts of neurological disorders—those were also inconclusive. Eventually, they determined that I might have multiple sclerosis after an MRI revealed a spot on my brain that apparently was reason enough for diagnosis. I remember the doctor calling me to tell me—trying to comfort me with words of encouragement.

This is where I move into the good part of the story.

During these hard months, I had been watching and digesting teachings from a televangelist named Andrew Womack. My mother had been watching him for a few years up until this point, and this teacher was unique in the fact that he believed it was God's will to heal. The man generally talked about the importance of faith in God's Word—believing that the Word revealed God's will to heal. He also generally discussed the power of "speaking to your mountain without doubt," a teaching outlined in Mark 11. A defining feature of this teaching, as Womack outlined it, was believing in a reception of healing from God before a tangible manifestation. I became convinced of this truth.

During these months, I began to fight the sickness by quite literally "speaking to my mountain," striving against all doubt to eradicate doubt. I spoke to the symptoms in my body. I spoke to the body parts that were not performing correctly. I cursed multiple sclerosis. I truly felt that these words were keeping me alive at the time. It was also during this time that some church elders at Crossroads Church of God in Jesup, Georgia, my uncle's church, prayed for my healing and anointed me with oil, which Scripture clearly commands the church to do for the sick. After this event, I began to experience dramatic improvement.

Upon starting to experience dramatic improvement, I got a second MRI on my brain. This was done to determine whether the "concerning spot" was still there; needless to say, it was gone! I have not experienced any episodes since that day at the church. I say all of this to say that God truly is a healing God. There is no other rational conclusion to come to. God healed me. I do not claim to have all of the answers regarding this topic. I do not claim to know everything there is to know about healing. I will say that I believe it is God's will to heal, however. I believe that "the word of faith" that I prayed during this time quite literally kept me going. As such, I pray that way for myself and other people in need of God's healing touch. I strongly encourage those that read this account to investigate the power of God further. You might be amazed by what you find and experience.

Chad Norris

Chad Norris is the great grandson of M. B. Norris. He currently is pursuing a master's degree from the Church of God Pentecostal Theological Seminary in Cleveland, Tennessee. He lives in Jesup, Georgia when not in school.

When I think about the legacy of my family, it has very much influenced the kind of person I wish to be. I am not aware of many of the finer details of my family's history as my father is, but I know enough to know that M. B. Norris was one of the finest examples of Christian men I have ever heard of.

When I heard the story of M. B. forgiving the man who killed his two boys in a drunk driving accident and then playing an instrumental role in getting that man released from prison, I wondered how many would be willing to do such a thing. Most would probably want to see that person punished and remain in jail for the rest of his life, but not M. B. He desired to see that person redeemed, made whole, and have a second chance at life again.

When I think of my grandfather, David Norris, who recently passed away in December 2020, he carried on the legacy of wanting to do good to people who did not want to do good to him. Although they were very different individuals in many ways, my grandfather exhibited many of the same traits as his father, particularly in wishing to see his family carry on in ministry, something that has also been encouraged by *my* father. I cannot tell you the number of times in the last few years my grandfather told me he looked forward to hearing me preach someday, and although I am still not sure if I *will* preach, I am excited about figuring out what God's call on my life is.

To put it simply, I am not sure I would be where I am today at Pentecostal Theological Seminary in Cleveland, Tennessee, if it were not for the influence of my family. I hope to make them proud. Family is a blessing, and I thank God for it every day.

Joel Allen Norris Sr.

As told by: Julia Stanley-Mack and Helen Johnson

Joel Allen Norris Sr. was an ordained Pentecostal minister and married Beatrice Cobb Anderson in 1947. He pastored, evangelized, and planted churches, along with his brother, M. B., in South Georgia, Florida, and Arkansas.

Joel Allen Norris Sr.

Joel Norris was born on November 22, 1894, to Reverend Preston Norris and Julia Lee. He came from a family of preachers. He, like two of his brothers, Marshall B. Norris and Foy Norris, were all ordained ministers and licensed in the Church of God. Not only was Joel an evangelist and pastor but a very talented songwriter, musician, and artist. It was in the Glennville, Georgia, Church of God, where he met Beatrice Cobb Anderson, who played the piano for the church services.

Joel and his brother M. B. Norris planted churches, often using their own funds to rent storefront buildings. Many of their revivals were held in tents with sawdust floors. The Norris brothers were well known by other churches in the surroundings areas of Southeast Georgia.

Following the revival in Glennville, Georgia, Bea and Joel began a correspondence relationship that evolved into a serious commitment. Joel's first wife, Gerre, had died of cancer two years earlier, and Beatrice had lost her husband, Palmer Anderson, to heart disease, leaving her with three small children. On January 10, 1947, in Jesup, Georgia, in the home of Joel's brother Harrison, the Reverend W. C. Swilley performed the marriage ceremony.

Harrison had four beautiful daughters. They lived in Jesup, Georgia, at that time. Betty, Barbara, Wanda, and Jessica, like others in the Norris family, they, too, traveled to surrounding churches and sang. Unlike his brothers, Harrison was not a minister; however, his life touched everyone around him with his kindness, compassion, gentle spirit, and infectious smile. He was truly a servant of the Lord.

Betty, Barbara, Wanda, and Jessica

After the wedding, Joel and Beatrice honeymooned with three of her children—Haven, Gerald, and Helen—at Cross City, Florida, where Joel conducted a revival. Beatrice's children were happy to begin their new lives with a new daddy! Shortly after the honeymoon, Joel and Bea began pastoring.

Joel's brother, Marshall, moved to Arkansas to become the state overseer for Church of God. He called and asked Joel to pastor the church in Earle. While the family was living in Earle, Arkansas, in November 1947, Joel Allen Jr. entered their home.

During Christmas 1948, the family enjoyed their first Christmas in the Ozarks; Joel took Haven, Gerald, and Helen through the snow into the woods behind the parsonage, where they picked out a pine tree to decorate. The prized tree was beautiful with only a few bulbs, pinecones, and the popcorn Mother helped us string. For several days, there were no gifts under the tree. Haven and Helen kept asking, "Where are all the presents?"

All the children grew anxious on a regular basis, asking about the gifts that should be under the tree. The answer was always the same from their parents, "They will be here; it's not Christmas yet!"

On Christmas Eve, the children went to bed with great excitement and wonder. Arising early on Christmas morning, they discovered a large cardboard box outside their front door. The gifts were beautifully wrapped and had each of their names on them. The angel who brought the gifts also brought a large turkey with all the trimmings and a Lane cake. Christmas in the Ozarks was one their family never forgot. They never knew where the gifts came from, but will always remember that God is never late!

"Every good and every perfect gift is from above and comes from the Father of lights, with whom is no variableness, neither shadow of turning" (James 1:17).

Two years later, Joel was called to pastor the Benton, Arkansas, Church of God. So, the family moved from Earle to Benton, and Julia Beatrice was born on March 14, 1949.

While Joel and his family were living in the Ozarks, they were around his brother, Marshall, and his family, who lived in Little Rock. The children looked forward to visiting them since both families had lived in Georgia. David Norris, Marshall's son, and Haven became close cousins. The two of them certainly knew how to play jokes on Haven's sister, Helen. Her red hair did not help at all! David was kind enough to teach her to ride a boy's bicycle. Yet, as hard as she tried to compete with her brother and cousin, she never mastered wheelies!

Joel was often called to preach in other churches around the state. He was asked to speak one Sunday night in a neighboring church some distance away. Traveling across the Ozark Mountains with rolling hills and valleys could be somewhat treacherous.

On this trip, Beatrice and five of their children accompanied him to the Sunday night service. Without warning, Joel lost control of the steering, and the car suddenly veered to the left, crossed the centerline, and came to rest against the mountainside. Joel immediately got out, accessed the damage, and determined the tie rod used for steering had come loose. As usual, he kept a bottle of olive oil in his pocket. He anointed the car with oil, prayed and thanked God for protection over his family, and asked God for safe travels down the mountain.

Arriving at the church, Joel gave thanks for a safe trip. He preached an evangelistic sermon, recounting his family's near disaster in getting down the mountain. The people at the church rejoiced, knowing it was nothing but a miracle that we arrived safely. Several souls were saved that evening as the Holy Spirit convicted their hearts. The greater miracle that Sunday was the salvation of souls! Early the next morning, the mechanic looked at the car with amazement and commented, "There's no way you could drive this car! It doesn't even have a tie rod in it. It's missing!" We could have veered into the deep ravine instead of the small ditch, but God had other plans!

"Because He hath set His love upon me, therefore will I deliver him: I will set him on high, because he hath known my name. He shall call upon me, and I will answer Him: I will be with him in trouble; I will deliver him, and honour him" **(Ps. 91:14).**

After pastoring in Arkansas for several years, Joel moved his family from Arkansas to Columbus, Georgia, in 1952. Ronald Preston was born there. When he was two years old, Ronald developed pneumonia, and the doctor was called to the family's house, where he gravely told Joel that it was too late to give Ronald a shot because he had no pulse.

Joel picked up his son, laid him on the table, and anointed him with oil. He then scooped Ronnie into his arms and walked around the room, asking God to heal him. Immediately, Ronnie cried out, and the doctor was amazed at the answer to his prayer. Two hours later, Ronnie was running around and playing!

This miracle happened on a Sunday morning. Daddy took him to church, and in front of the congregation, announced, "I want you to see a baby that saw God and heaven this morning, but God sent him back to us! To God be the glory!"

While we were living in Columbus, Joel's daughter, Kate, by his first wife, Gerre, decided to visit her dad and meet his new family. Kate was a beautiful girl in her late twenties, with long hair and a wonderful smile. She was married to John Shipe, and they had three children: Freda, Paul, and Johnny. They made their home in Baltimore, Maryland.

Kate's plans were to stay a couple of weeks with her dad, but that didn't happen. After a couple of days sharing her stories with her dad about their lives in Baltimore, Kate began to feel ill and came down with a high fever, a stiff neck, a rash, and blotchy skin. Joel called his brother, Marshall, who was pastoring in Columbus at that time, and he and the elders of his church came to our house to pray for Kate. They anointed her with oil, as the Bible teaches.

When the doctor came to the house, he gave the sad news that Kate had meningitis, a highly contagious disease that required being quarantined. Kate was immediately admitted to the hospital and placed in the intensive care unit. The doctor told Joel that his daughter probably wouldn't make it, and Kate's husband in Baltimore should be called. Joel, however, was relentless in praying for her.

"And the prayer of faith shall save the sick, and if he hath committed sin, they shall be forgiven" (James 5:15).

God was not done! He performed a miracle for Kate, restored her faith in God, and she was reunited with her family in Baltimore. Several years later, Kate's son Paul was healed after being prayed for by the late Oral Roberts.

"The God of my rock; in him will I trust: He is my shield, and the horn of my salvation, my high tower, and my refuge, my savior; thou savest me from violence" (2 Sam. 22:3).

It was in Boykin that Joel and his family lived next door to the church. Their daughter, Gloria, was born there, then Joel and Beatrice moved from Boykin to Colquitt, Georgia, to plant a new Church of God church. Joel started by having services in his family's home. After a few months, he bought a tent and put it up on an empty lot between his house on Pine Street and a huge peanut silo.

Southwest Georgia was called the Peanut Capital. The major crops were peanuts and cotton. In the summer, all the children old enough to work went to the fields to pick cotton. Julie was six years old and pulled and picked cotton with Helen, who was fifteen at the time. Most of the offerings received went back into the work of the ministry. When he wasn't pastoring, Joel worked on the side as a salesman, and his wife taught piano lessons. There were several preachers that came out of that church in Colquitt from Joel's ministry.

Each year, Joel took his family to Camp Meeting at the Doraville campus. They stayed in a small cabin near the tabernacle. Beatrice would spend days getting the children's clothes prepared along with food to take and other necessities.

One particular year, Joel was invited to speak at the early morning service at Camp Meeting. Beatrice observed that Joel had a hole in the sole of one of his dress shoes. She told him he needed a new pair of shoes before Camp Meeting. He shined his shoes and later told her, "Bea, I can wear these shoes. We need the money we have for the week in Doraville. God knows if I need shoes, He can take care of that. He will send them to me, **even if they have to come from Russia!**"

Earlier that year, Joel had a missionary visit his church in Donaldsonville, Georgia. The missionary was on furlough to raise funds for his assigned work on the mission field. He stayed in Joel's home, preached a mission message in his church, and spoke about his missionary work. Joel received an offering for him for his mission work.

A few days before Joel's family left for Camp Meeting, a very large box from California arrived at their door from this same missionary. Included in the box was a letter that read, "Bro Norris, we are preparing to return to the mission field, and have exceeded the number of pounds of supplies we are allowed to ship. God spoke to me this morning and told me to send this extra box to you and your family. I hope you will be able use the contents."

As the family opened the box, there were children's clothes of various sizes. And there, in the very bottom of the box, underneath the clothes, was a pair of men's dress shoes, size ten. On the inside of the shoes, the inscription read "MADE IN RUSSIA."

We will tell of His mighty acts and praise His wondrous works. God hears every word we speak!

In 1957, the family moved to Savannah, where Joel continued to evangelize. He worked in restoring old upright pianos, then sold them to supplement the family income. He also continued to work for L. B. Price Company and run revivals as Beatrice continued to teach piano lessons. In the fall of that year, their family moved to Cherokee Lakes, outside Jesup, Georgia, and later to a larger house in Madray Springs, a small community thirteen miles from Jesup. Joel's health was deteriorating, and the older children worked in the fields to help with the household necessities.

In 1960, the family traveled to Michigan for the summer, and Joel scheduled revivals in the Benton Harbor area for Reverend Ricketts and Reverend Chapin. Reverend Chapin was also a judge and good friend of Joel's. All the children enjoyed working in the fruit fields picking cherries, blueberries, and strawberries. It was really a fun summer when Joel's brother, Harrison, and his family joined them. At the close of summer, the family returned to Georgia for the children to start a new school year.

Joel became bedfast in 1962; it was a very challenging year for the family. During the winter, they burned wood in the fireplaces. There were no bathtubs or hot running water. The house originally was an old store building; an addition in the rear provided several extra bedrooms. There were no closets, and the wooden floors had cracks in them.

The Norris Brothers and Their Spouses

During this time, Beatrice was very strong, but it was an enormous challenge raising boys without her husband's help. Thankfully, Marshall, Harrison, and Foy assisted their sister-in-law by taking the children to live with them for the summer. Christians in the area churches and family members were very kind to see the family's needs were met. This allowed Joel to remain at home while Beatrice nursed him around the clock.

He died on January 22, 1963, still trusting God with unwavering **faith**. What a legacy of faith!

"I have fought a good fight, I have finished the race, I have kept the faith: Henceforth, there is laid up for me a crown of righteousness, which the Lord, the righteous judge, shall give me at that day: and not to me only, but unto all them also that love his appearing" (2 Tim. 4:7–8).

What a legacy of faith to leave his children.

"That if thou shalt confess with thy mouth the Lord Jesus, and shalt believe in thine heart that God hath raised Him from the dead, thou shall be saved" (Rom. 10:9).

Joel Allen Norris Jr. (J. A.)

Joel was the firstborn to Joel Norris Sr. and Beatrice Norris. He is the father of two daughters, Pam and Becky. Though they will never know their father, one day, they will know their heritage.

Joel Allen Norris Jr. (J. A.)

Joel was very talented in cabinet making. He had just been discharged from the hospital, recovering from kidney surgery. He had promised Julia, his sister, he would make her a picture frame for a map of the world. He was at her home, measuring for the frame, when, suddenly, he had sharp pains in his kidney area. He grabbed his side and collapsed in Julia's arms. He passed away while they were praying together. He loved the Bible and had an excellent command of the Scriptures. From his training in the home, he could quote many passages and left a testimony. He was an excellent singer with a baritone voice.

"Oh how I love thy law! It is my meditation all the day. Thou through thy commandments hast made me wise" (**Ps. 119:97**).

Julia Beatrice Norris Stanley-Mack

Julia (Julie) Beatrice Norris Stanley-Mack, is the first daughter of Joel Allen Sr. and Beatrice Norris. She has pastored Life Spring Worship Center in Bloomingdale, Georgia, for thirty-seven years. She is a certified counselor with the American Association of Christian Counselors. For the past twenty-three years, she has served as the administrator of LSCA, a state-accredited Academy. She is the founder and president of Master's College of Georgia (training for men and women in biblical studies and equipping them for ministry). She is the director of a local FM gospel radio station in its fifth year. She is a singer, musician, and is often asked to speak at women's conferences and Camp Meetings. She is a mother of three, Billy Stanley Jr., Shannon Terrell, and Chelby Seckinger. She is also a grandmother of six. She is married to Billy Mack.

Julia Mack and Billy Mack

I was born on March 14, 1949, to the Reverend Joel Allen Norris Sr. and Beatrice Cobb Norris in Benton, Arkansas, where my dad pastored. My daddy said he named me after the two most beautiful women he knew: my paternal grandmother, and my mother, Beatrice. When I was born, I was number five in the pecking order. Joel Allen Jr. was less than two years older than me.

Chelby Seckinger, Billy Stanley Jr., and Shannon Terrell

I grew up in a home where faith in God and the Word was central to our existence. These values are what formed me into the person I am today and propelled me into my ministry. I saw my father pray for the sick, and they recovered. He was known throughout his ministry as a faith preacher. Healing was not only manifested in our home but in the public square, hospitals, and the homes of his church members. He was creative and very talented the way he presented the Scriptures in our home. His desire was that all his children know Christ as their Lord and Savior.

"For by grace are ye saved by faith; and that not of yourself: it is the gift of God: Not of works, lest any should boast" (Eph. 2:8–9).

When he was preparing his sermons, he would call all the children (who could read) to sit on the floor before him with a Bible. We learned to recite the books of the Bible by singing them from Genesis to Revelation. He played a game called Scripture Scramble with us, where he would call out scripture for us to look up and read. These were scriptures that he would incorporate in his sermons; he would write his sermon notes while we competed to be the first to locate the Bible scripture. **We were getting the Word in our hearts without realizing it.**

Alaina and Kenzie Terrell

Parents, how clever is that? As a child, I was the recipient of God filling my heart with His Word and preparing me for my future ministry. **What a legacy Daddy left for his children.**

I memorized the Word and learned to love God during these sessions. There were times Daddy would call us up front and have us recite what we had learned.

We will tell of God's greatness and faithfulness to the next generation.

Chelby Lynn Seckinger with Joel and Carly

My father, Joel Norris, instilled in me a love for the Word, and I have learned Psalm 119:11 is true, ***"Thy word have I hid in my heart that I might not sin against Thee."***

When we had questions about why we couldn't do something, Daddy would always explain the reason based on God's Word. We would sit down and see what the Word said about that question. This practice was also demonstrated when we got in trouble. Before he punished us, he would pray with us and tell us that he loved us and wanted others to love us. Mother did not operate so much in the same spirit when she disciplined us. She believed in swift punishment ...not always with prayer and Bible reading like Daddy.

My parents told me when I was born, I had a clubfoot; a clubfoot is a bone development disease. Daddy called for the people of the church to pray for me. A doctor diagnosed me and told my parents to take me to Little Rock to a specialist who could operate. I would wear a brace and possibly walk by the time I started school. When the doctor reported this, Mother started crying. Daddy said to Mother, "Before we go to Little Rock, let's pray one more time for this baby."

He anointed my cripple foot and put me to bed. The next morning, Mother went in to check on me and called Daddy into my room. During the night, I was completely healed! We often hear the devil does his work at night, but I am here to testify my healing occurred during the night, proving God is the God of the night, and he doesn't slumber nor sleep.

***"Behold, the Protector of Israel will neither slumber nor sleep"* (Ps. 121:4).**

God heard my parents' prayer, and during the night gave us a miracle! One would never know I had a defective foot when I walk or speak, wearing three-inch heels.

Early Ministry of Billy and Julia Stanley

Ronald "Ronnie" P. Norris

Ronald Preston Norris is the second son born to Joel Allen Norris Sr. and Beatrice Cobb Norris. He is married to Ritsuko Norris, and they have two children, Yuki (deceased) and Rick. Ronald is a retired professional land surveyor, having worked in that profession for over twenty years.

Celebrating 50 years of Love!

Ronnie and Ritsuko Norris

I was born in Columbus, Georgia, on August 2, 1950. I don't have any recollection of my days in Columbus, but at some point at that period of my life, I had a traumatic situation where I was believed to have had double pneumonia. I ran an extremely high fever, and my parents were told that I had succumbed to death. I've heard this story many times in my life, but I will leave it to be told by others. My parents and others were there and recall the details. That could be called the first miracle of many in my life.

Haven Anderson Sr. – Air Force Proud

I loved growing up with lots of brothers and sisters in my home. I loved them all, but my first sad experience was when my oldest brother, Haven, joined the Air Force. He was preparing for basic training. I was really close to him and heartbroken to hear he was leaving. I was around five years old, and I hid in the rear floorboard of the car. As Dad was taking him to the bus station, I got caught and had to stay home. I felt he was going away forever.

That summer, our family took a summer trip to Michigan to work in the cherry orchards and blueberry fields. We used the money we earned for our back-to-school clothes and new shoes. Once the summer was over, we moved to Colquitt, Georgia. Then, for reasons unknown to me, we moved to Punta Gorda, Florida, where I started my first grade of school. I don't really recall a lot about Punta Gorda, but I seemed to be doing well in school. We had been in school several months when my parents decided to move back to Georgia, this time to Savannah. The second half of that school year was not that great for me. I had a slight speech impediment and was very self-conscious about it. My new teacher had no patience with me. When she would call on me to read or just to converse with me, she would mock me, and I would become nervous and begin to stutter. She then would tell me to sit down. I think that destroyed my self-confidence, and I really dreaded to be called on. With encouragement from my mom, I was able to make it through the school year with only my pride hurt ...and no permanent damage.

During the summer of that year, we moved again, this time, to Jesup, Georgia, to a rural community known as The Crossroads. I attended the Piney Grove Elementary School. Things there seemed pretty good for me, and I found out that I liked country living much better than city living. We also had relatives living in that vicinity, both on my mother's side and my father's side. We had lots of cousins and lots of fun sleeping over at one another's houses. The kids would make pallets on the floor, and we would stay awake most of the night, horse playing and telling scary stories.

That summer, along with my brothers, sisters, and cousins, we worked in the field of Uncle Marshall's farm. One day, we decided to go to the pond to cool off. At the pond, my older cousin, David Norris, instructed me to stay at the shallow end of the pond while the older boys were wrestling and playing at the opposite end of the pond, which was much deeper.

At one point, I decided to join the others at the deep end without their knowledge. The water at the deep end was well over my head, and I had not learned to swim. Suddenly, I found myself bouncing off the bottom and coming to the surface to yell for help, only to take in a mouthful of pond water and sink again. At some point, my cousin David noticed me floundering in the water and was able to pull me to safety. I must have swallowed half the pond, plus I got a good scolding. That was another miracle in my life that I can remember.

I had now considered looking at Jesup as my home, and still today, I call Jesup home. At the end of that summer, we moved again—back to Savannah. There I attended the third, fourth, fifth, and sixth grades. There was not a lot of excitement in those days except the normal growing up with school friends, summer jobs, like mowing grass, and sometimes a weekend trip back to Jesup to visit our relatives. I really looked forward to those short weekend visits.

At the end of my sixth-grade year, we moved back to Jesup to a little community called Cherokee Lakes. Once again, we moved to another little community called Madray Springs. Just as before, I found myself loving everything about the country compared to living in the city. Hey, it was good to be back home again. Once again, it was good to be able to hang out with my cousins and friends.

My mom's family lived in Glennville, Georgia, about thirty minutes away, and on occasion, we would visit them. I really cherished those days when we would go visit my maternal grandfather and grandmother.

Sometime in 1962, my dad became ill and spent a lot of time in bed. He was too ill to get out of bed. On the good days, he was able to get up and make sure we had a garden growing. He would teach my older brother, J. A., and me how to plow and work it. Other times during the summer, when he was able, the whole family would work for the farmer that also owned a little country store. We would work off the debt we had accumulated over the last several months. As sick as my dad was, he managed to carry his weight working on the farm. During this time of his sickness, he allowed me to practice driving. I had just turned twelve, and my dad would already let me drive him to church using the back roads, and he occasionally allowed me to drive on the highway. For some reason, the rest of the family decided not to go with us.

January 22, 1963, as I was getting ready for school, Dad asked if I would get an old-style church fan and fan him while he was lying in bed. Because we didn't have air conditioning in the house, he would have some of the other children also fan him. His health was deteriorating, and it was obvious that he was in extreme pain. I remember fanning him one morning while waiting for the school bus. One could see the school bus coming and making other stops on the way. My dad asked if

I would fan him, and I recall fanning him until one of my siblings yelled that the bus was coming. My dad asked if I would fan him until the bus arrived. I remember complaining that I might miss the bus. He told me that he might not be home when I got out of school. I continued fanning until someone yelled that the bus was here, and I rushed out of the house to meet the bus.

It was mid-morning that same day the principal came into my classroom. He walked over to my teacher and had a short conversation with her. As the principal left the room, my teacher came to my desk and told me to gather my belongings because I was needed at home. It was the middle of January, and I had taken my shoes off at the earlier recess. She grabbed my shoes and led me to the principal's office.

When I arrived at the principal's office, I saw the principal of the school where my older brother J. A. attended. Joining me there were my two older sisters and younger brother. The principal said he was taking us all home. As we got into his car, J. A. sat in the front passenger's seat, reading a book. At this point, we only knew we were going home.

When we arrived home, Mama Cobb had picked up my older sister, who was a senior in her last quarter at Georgia Southern University in Statesboro, Georgia, and we all were met at the door by the pastor of the Blanton Grove Church of God. He gave us the devastating news that our dad had passed away. He was there to comfort us and pray with us.

The words my dad had spoken to me that morning lay heavily on my heart. He must have known that this would be his last day on earth. That was really hard on every one of us. Since I was the emotional one, and I was only twelve years old, I believe I took it the worst. I probably didn't realize how much it affected my mother, for now, she was a widow with five and sometimes six children at home to worry about and help pull us through this tragedy. She was an incredibly strong Christian woman, and her faith in God would surely pave a way forward for us.

Brothers: Ronnie, Philip, and Gerald

After the death of my dad, my mom decided it would be more advantageous to move back to Savannah, where the job opportunities would be a lot better for her. She had previously enrolled in nursing school. J. A. had decided that rather than go to Savannah with the family, he would finish his senior year with some longtime family friends in Lyons, Georgia. It was only about an hour from Savannah, which made it convenient for him to come home quite frequently. In Lyons, he could finish high school and work for the Morris family on their farm. The LeRoy Morris family had known my mom and dad for many years and had invited J. A. to come stay with them for his senior year. They had a daughter about the same age as J. A., and I believe that had a lot to do with his decision. Mom gave him her blessing, and off he went to Lyons. J. A. graduated with honors, and we were so proud of him.

Over the next few years, Mom worked many, many hours, including double shifts, to give us children a good life. As difficult as it was, she tried very hard to be both a mother and father. My older brother, Gerald, decided he would stay in Jesup after Daddy died. Now there was J. A. in Lyons and Gerald in Jesup. That left Julie, Gloria, Philip, and me at home.

J. A., Ronnie, Bea, Philip, Gloria, and Julia

After returning to Savannah that next summer, Mom decided we would once again travel to Michigan to work in the blueberry and cherry farms. This would allow us to earn money to pay off some debts and earn money to buy school clothes for the upcoming school year.

After the summer and upon returning home to Savannah, we were immediately approached by a neighbor who informed us about my best friend, who was killed the night before while riding as a passenger on a motorcycle. He was traveling from Savannah Beach on the back of the motorcycle when someone hit them from the rear, knocking them out into the marsh and not stopping to offer help. Someone came along, saw the motorcycle next to the road, assumed there must be someone nearby, and then found the driver. As the ambulance transported the driver to the hospital, he awoke long enough to ask about his passenger. They radioed back to the scene and alerted the law that there was a passenger involved. After searching the marsh area, they found my friend in the swamp, deceased. The driver ended up passing away when they reached the hospital. This was another tragedy and shock to me.

Growing up in Savannah the next couple of years was rather boring; getting my driver's license, going to the beach, working part-time, and going to school pretty much sums up my life during that time. Mom still worked two jobs most of the time. She did her best to give us a good home and keep us in line. She would also take us to church whenever possible.

As I grew older, I began to think I knew everything and didn't need my mother's guidance. I started to hang out with a group of kids not raised in Christian homes. My best friend was Raymond, who was from a broken home. His dad drank a lot, and he did not live with his mother. So, Raymond often bounced between staying with his mother, father, and our house.

One day, Raymond and I decided to skip school. Later that day, we began to worry about getting into trouble for skipping school. One of us suggested that we run away from home. Neither of us had a penny to our name. I talked him into going where I called home—Jesup. I told him that we could hop a freight train that would take us there. I had done that before, but I couldn't remember which train to hop. We were lucky, for the train we took was the right one. The train always stopped in Jesup, hooked more cars, and left some behind. I knew the train would be there for quite a while. Once in Jesup, we had to hitch-hike out to the country where I had lived years earlier. I guess I was hoping to see some old friends or just stay in some farmer's old haybarn.

While walking down an old dirt road in the country, a station wagon stopped and offered us a ride. The driver of the car was named Dale. He was the older brother of a schoolmate I hadn't seen for several years. I explained that we had run away from Savannah and were going to look for jobs in that area. He told us that he was living in Wilson, North Carolina, and was only visiting Jesup for a few days. He said he was leaving Jesup immediately, heading home to North Carolina, where he worked at a truck stop. He offered to take us with him if we wanted, and we could ride with him and look for a job there. After a short discussion, we decided to head for North Carolina. Along the way, Dale stopped and bought hamburgers for us. That was the first thing we had to eat since leaving home earlier that morning. We finally arrived at the truck stop where Dale worked. He worked late at night and slept in a backroom. He offered his car for us to sleep in.

The next day, Dale bought us breakfast and a newspaper so we could check the job section in the want ads. There was one restaurant looking for a dishwasher. Dale took us there; Raymond and I both applied for the job, only to find out that the job had already been filled. With Dale having to return to work, we walked the streets for some time looking for Help Wanted signs. Later that day, I told Raymond I had a brother in the Air Force in Ohio, and we could go there. Away we went hitchhiking in a northerly direction. We had no idea how to get to Columbus, Ohio. To this day, I have no idea how I knew the street or suburb Haven lived on. I just remembered the name was Reynoldsburg. Possibly, we had passed through there on one of our many trips with Mom to Michigan.

As we headed in a northerly direction toward Ohio with no money to eat and only a long-sleeved shirt on our backs, the weather began to get really cold. As night approached, we really wished we were back in Georgia. We were even hoping a lawman would come by so we could turn ourselves in as runaways, just to get out of the cold. Later that night, as we were walking along a highway in either Virginia or West Virginia, we came to a gas station that had closed for the night. There was a coke machine outside by the doorway, so Raymond checked the change return and found a dime someone had left. Boy, did we feel we had hit the jackpot on a slot machine.

As the night grew, we came across a bowling alley where we thought would be a good place to get out of the cold, hoping maybe at closing we could catch a ride with someone leaving. With that dime Raymond found in the coke machine, we were each able to have a pack of crackers with complimentary glasses of water from the snack bar. We took our sweet time eating those crackers, even though we were starving. We just needed to stay in the warmth and comfort of the bowling alley for as long as possible. As the alley began to close, we walked out to the highway with our thumbs out, hoping to hitch a ride north. After about an hour and no rides, it seemed that everyone had gone, and we were left there in the dark, still freezing.

We noticed there was a Jeep truck left in the parking lot of the bowling alley, so we waited a little longer to see if anyone else came out. After a while, we were satisfied that everyone had left, and we thought whoever left the Jeep must have had too much to drink and had caught a ride home. As we approached the Jeep, we realized the door was not locked, so we got in out of the cold to try to sleep for the rest of the night. Raymond got in the driver's seat, and I got in the passenger's side. Soon, Raymond realized that someone had left the keys in the ignition, so he started the engine and found the heater that eventually heated the cabin. We warmed ourselves up good and then turned the engine off until we got cold again. To us, it felt as though we were in the Holiday Inn. We continued running the engine off and on until daylight, at which time we left the comfort of the Jeep and headed back into the cold, going north. By then, we thought about turning around, but it was farther to go back to Savannah, Georgia, than to continue toward Columbus, Ohio.

Another day on the road, catching rides, mostly for short distances, and a lot of walking found us exhausted. As another night fell in the mountains of West Virginia, we found ourselves walking along a country road with snow flurries. At some point, we came upon a house in the countryside that was dark. It looked to us as if everyone had gone to bed. There was a car parked by the house and an older car a little farther away, which appeared to be an old junk car. We made our way to the old junk car, got in quietly, and decided to spend the night there. Lucky for us, no one saw or shot us. We were so cold the latter would have been fine. Not as comfortable as the previous night, but we had a place to rest and were out of the wind and snow. The next morning, we arose and checked out by daylight to get an early start and get away before the landlord got up and wanted to collect the rent.

Later in the day, we caught a ride with a guy in a box-type moving van. After small talk, he told us he was traveling from Naples, Florida, but I didn't recall where he was going. I mentioned that my sister had married a guy from Naples. He asked my brother-in-law's name, and I mentioned Brian Johnson. He told me he knew Brian quite well, for they had worked together at the Beachcomber Hotel. This really was a small world. He dropped us off later in the afternoon in Columbus. Now we needed to find where Reynoldsburg was located and get a ride there. We found a city map at a gas station and were able to locate the street my brother lived on.

As it turned out, we caught a ride with someone who knew the area well, and he was kind enough to drop us off on Haven's street. Now came the task of beginning to knock on doors, seeking my brother or someone who might know him. We spent quite a while knocking on doors with no clues of where he lived. Finally, someone told me of an Air Force family who lived two doors down. As we knocked on the door, the gentleman opened the door, but he was not the person I was looking for. As I explained who I was looking for, he said there was a Sergeant Anderson down the street, so off we went. Someone answered the door, telling us this was the Anderson's residence but not Haven Anderson.

As I knocked on another house door farther down the street, a Volkswagen Bug pulled into the driveway. Several military men were in the car, and as they were unloading, I asked the driver if he knew Sgt. Haven Anderson. Before he could answer, Haven got out of the back-seat. Boy, was I glad to see him. He asked where I had been; Mom had called the day I left home and told him I may be headed to Columbus. As usual, my mother was a step ahead of me. We were really glad to get a hot meal and shower with clean clothes. I was especially glad to see Haven and his wife Ruth. After a couple of weeks with Haven and Ruth, Haven took some time off and drove us back to Savannah. At the least, it was a good learning experience that I will never forget or repeat. Our trip back was long and uneventful, but much better than our trip up.

One night a month or so after returning to Savannah, I was sitting in a pizza shop on Main Street when my friend Dale came walking through the door. He was the guy that had given Raymond and me a ride to North Carolina. He was moving back to Savannah to find a job and needed a place to stay. My mom had rented a three-story older home, which had extra rooms on the third floor that we never used, so she agreed to rent a room to him.

Dale asked me if I wanted to hitchhike to North Carolina with him on Friday to get his car, which he had left there until he could find a place to park it. I agreed, and late Friday afternoon after he finished work, we took off. By now, I felt I was a pro at thumbing down the highway. We thumbed most of the night or at least till after midnight and realized that most of the traffic had stopped for the night.

We later came across a truck stop and went inside to get something to eat and drink. We drank coffee until daylight. As we began thumbing, one of the first vehicles to come by was an ambulance. The driver stopped and offered us a ride. A ride is a ride, but we just didn't know what a ride would be. The driver explained that he owned the ambulance but had been working for another ambulance company out of town. He had worked the night before and was headed home for the weekend. He said he was very tired, and we noticed he was driving very fast. I was sitting by the door, and Dale was in the middle. As we approached traffic, the driver would turn on his red lights so all the traffic would move to the right to allow us to pass. I would occasionally look over toward the speedometer, and I once noticed that he was traveling ninety to one hundred fifteen miles per hour. He definitely had the petal to the metal as we flew up Interstate 85.

"He that dwelleth in the secret place of the most high shall abide under the shadow of the Almighty" (**Ps. 91:1**).

I looked ahead and saw a curve we were approaching, but I knew we had time to slow before entering the curve. As I looked at the speedometer again, we were traveling one hundred fifteen miles per hour. I looked at the driver and realized he was taking a nap. Before I could say anything, he awoke and began applying the brakes, which caused us to fishtail and swerve as we rounded the curve. When we exited the curve, we entered a bridge, where we hit the bridge curb on the driver's side, then the passenger's side. I have no idea how fast we were going, but it was faster than he could handle. We then hit the backside of a semi-truck with my side of the ambulance. I certainly wanted out but never saw a getting-out place. We then slid off the road on the driver's side and went down a steep embankment, rolling the ambulance two and a half times before a cluster of hardwoods stopped us and prevented us from going all the way to the bottom of a ravine. No one was wearing a seat belt; we all ended up on the driver's side trying to exit through the passenger's window.

Finally, we all got out, making sure we were okay. We made our way to the top of the hill, where a couple of semi-trucks had stopped and were putting out flares to warn the oncoming traffic. I'm not sure the truck we hit even stopped, but one of the other truck drivers asked if we were all okay. The ambulance driver said to Dale and me, "Let's get our story straight before the law arrives. Tell him that we were only doing sixty-five or seventy miles per hour."

One of the truck drivers overheard the conversation and commented, "Mister, I was going ninety miles per hour when you flew by me, but say what you want."

When the state trooper arrived and learned what had happened according to the ambulance driver's statement, he then verified everyone was okay. He had another state trooper take Dale and me to a truck stop further up the road in the direction we were traveling. Once we were there, we continued our trip thumbing up the road. We finally arrived at our destination later that evening. We slept in Dale's car that night, which was parked at the truck stop where he had previously worked. The next day, we left and headed back to Savannah. I have to say thanks to a mother who prayed all the time for us, for we definitely had someone looking out for us.

Later that summer, I decided that I was a man and wanted to join the Army. I was only sixteen and still needed my mother's signature. One month after I turned seventeen, my mom gave in and provided her permission for me to enlist. I think my mom wanted to get me away from my surroundings. I had asked my hobo friend Raymond to join me so we could go to basic training on the buddy plan. He wanted no part of military, so I went alone.

Away I went to Fort Gordon, Georgia. After about a month into my basic training, I received a letter from my mother telling me about my friend Raymond with whom I had run away to Ohio. He had been involved in a fight with an older man in Savannah, and the man had been killed. Raymond had been charged with his death. Again, my mom had been right about the friends that I chose. As I read her letter,

I realized what she had been warning me about, and now I could see why she finally gave in to my desire to join the Army. She must have had bad feelings about me staying in Savannah.

After a couple of months at Fort Gordon, I was sent to Fort Dix, New Jersey, for the next phase of my training. There I got another dose of snow, which I had not seen since my trip to Ohio, almost a year earlier. I was able to go home for a couple of weeks around Christmas and enjoy the warm Georgia weather, but after that, back to the cold in New Jersey.

After my time there, I went to Fort Benning in Columbus, Georgia, for my airborne training. Funny after seventeen years, here I was back to where it all started, my place of birth. After graduation, I became a US Army paratrooper.

The next duty station was Fort Bragg, North Carolina, home of the 82nd Airborne Division. Shortly after arriving, we were told to retrieve our personal belongings and military gear and return to the formation area in one hour; our unit was being deployed to Vietnam. It seemed as though we were leaving immediately without even being able to call home. I had heard that you had to be eighteen to go to Vietnam, but I guess someone forgot to tell our commanders.

After returning with our gear, we were told if our name was called, we should line up in a different formation. As we all waited and listened for our names, mine was finally called. After they finished calling names, they explained that the following people should be in our formation: anyone who had only been back from Vietnam for less than two months, anyone having less than six months in the Army, and lastly, anyone less than eighteen years old. Then they told us that we would not be going to Vietnam.

I spent the next eighteen months jungle training in preparation for Vietnam; there was also some training for riot control, if needed, stateside. After eighteen months, I finally got my orders for Vietnam. All military personnel would, sooner or later, get orders with the exception of those who had special or unusual circumstances. After my leave, I reported to Oakland, California, then to Vietnam, stopping on Wake Island in the Pacific.

Everyone on the chartered plane enjoyed the flight and seemed to have a good time until we got over Vietnam and began our decent through the clouds. You could see bomb craters everywhere you looked and smoke rising from below. Everyone on the flight got very quiet. We took our seats to spend time alone with our thoughts. It was an eerie feeling, but I believe everyone on board had the same emotions, even the ones returning for their second or third tour.

We arrived at Bien Hoa Airbase. Haven, my older brother, was serving his time in Vietnam in the Air Force at Tan Son Nhut Air Force base in nearby Saigon. We had a couple of hours at the airbase before we could get transportation to Long Bien Army Reception Center, not too far away.

While waiting, I was able to reach Haven by phone. He said he could be there in thirty minutes or so. He arrived at the airport, where we waited for a few minutes. I was extremely happy to see him since he had always been my favorite brother. After our short reunion, busses with armed security took us to the Army Reception Center at Long Bien. Here we processed in and were sent to our assigned areas of the country and our unit. My orders were to go north of Saigon, a couple of hundred miles to the 173rd Airborne Division.

We were asked at a reception if we had any family members in the country and if we wanted to be near them. Several of us answered yes, and the remainder were taken to the airfield nearby in a helicopter or small cargo plane to their perspective bases. The rest of us spent that night in Long Bien, which gave the brass time to reassign us to a base close to our family as we had requested.

The next day, I was sent to Tay Ninh Base Camp about fifty miles Northwest of Saigon, near the Cambodian border, to the 25th Infantry Division. While checking in at the base, us new guys got our first taste of combat in Vietnam. Within ten minutes of arriving, we received several rockets near our location. The first rocket hit nearby, and my first instinct, along with most of the new arrivals, was to hit the ground. The sergeant briefing us laughed and said that was our artillery firing outward and told us we would soon be able to distinguish outgoing from incoming fire.

About that time, another rocket hit within a few hundred feet from us, and the sergeant was down on top of us. No more laughing at the new boys. After several more rockets were heard landing farther away, the attack ended. We were told that every time the enemy sees or hears a plane landing, they always fire rockets in our direction, hoping to get lucky and hit the plane, the fuel, or ammo dump. This time, lucky for us, no one got injured.

That afternoon, an armored personnel carrier arrived at camp for resupply, then they returned to the Fire Support Base about ten miles out from where they worked. That would be my ride to my base where I worked. Every morning, we would leave the firebase to patrol the area outside our perimeter and around the base of a large mountain called Nui Ba Dien, where the enemy was known to have their own base deep underground within the mountain.

The US Army controlled the top and bottom of the mountain, and the enemy controlled the middle. We also pulled security for our firebase, using their large guns. They then would support our infantry when we were in trouble and needed artillery support. Mostly, we went out early in the am, sometimes as a whole company of 125 men, and other times as a platoon of about 25 to 30 men. We patrolled the area near our base while looking for any activities, such as tunnels, spider holes, and any other unusual things. Other times, we took turns going out at night to set up ambushes to deter enemy activity trying to penetrate our perimeter.

"Though I walk in the midst of trouble, thou wilt revive me: Thou shalt stretch forth thine hand against the wrath of thine enemies and thy right hand shall save me" (**Ps. 138:7**).

After several weeks in the field, under very stressful conditions, each platoon would rotate to the rear base camp at Tay Ninh for a three-day stand down, simply to relax and get our minds off the constant being on alert. As our platoon went to the rear for our stand down, I asked someone, "If I wanted to go to Saigon, how would I get there?"

I was told if I stood just outside the guard gate, there would always be armed convoys leaving our base or others coming by from other bases, heading to Saigon. Next to our base was a major highway. I decided I would hitchhike my way to Saigon since I was really good at hitchhiking. After just a short time standing outside the gate, a convoy came by.

With my thumb out, the convoy came to a halt, and the commander of the lead truck told me to get in the last truck. Fortunately, all the soldiers in the trucks turned out to be South Vietnamese, but after all, we were there to help them, so I felt I could trust them. With my weapon over my shoulder, I climbed aboard, and away we went to Saigon so I could visit my brother, Haven. Luckily, the convoy was going to the airbase where Haven worked.

Soon I arrived at Haven's office. He worked alongside another N.C.O., a captain, and a major. I walked in unannounced straight from the field wearing my jungle fatigues that I had already been wearing for several days and my weapon over my shoulder. The office group was wearing a dress-type uniform. I looked as though I had just come out of a Rambo movie.

Soon Haven realized who I was and looked a little embarrassed but introduced me to everyone. Masterly he teased me a bit about being a grunt, a nickname for one who spends his time in the jungle. This nickname usually applied to Army soldiers with no special training or useful skills other than combat. Haven took the rest of the day off and took me into Saigon, where he was living. The Air Force had leased a hotel, which was heavily fortified both on the perimeter of the ground and on the roof.

There, Haven changed from his uniform into civilian clothes, and we left the hotel to go out on the town. We rode a moped that had been converted into a taxi with a double seat that extended in front of the driver. The traffic was crazy with no traffic lights or stop signs. I thought if we were to get hit, we were in front of the driver, and therefore, we would catch the blunt of the impact. It was rather scary, but the drivers were very courteous to each other, and we made the trip without incident.

We went to a large three-story open apartment building to the second floor, where a very pretty young lady and small child lived. Haven introduced the lady as his tour guide and laundry lady and explained to me that everyone had a person that took care of laundry, shoes, and boot shines. He also explained that anything he needed from the Vietnamese black market, she could get for him because she was street-wise and knowledgeable. Haven gave her some money, and she left for the market to purchase something for our dinner. She returned in about a half-hour with the biggest shrimp I had ever seen.

The stove in the apartment was located in the hallway, where it was shared with other tenants. Waiting for her turn to cook, Haven and I sat down to relax and talk about home and family. The apartment was wide open with a couple of fans for comfort. When she finished cooking, we sat down for a meal like I had not eaten in a long time. The shrimp took up most of my plate, and they were delicious.

Haven explained that he had a military roommate back at his hotel, and he had nowhere for me to stay; however, his lady friend said I could stay there in the bed against the wall on the far side of the large, one-room apartment. Haven and I hung a blanket for a curtain around my bed for privacy. Soon Haven left for his hotel for the night and said he would see me the next day after his work, but the lady would take me around Saigon sightseeing and to the open market the next day. It was very interesting, to say the least. I had a very pretty guide that entertained me.

That evening as we were having dinner, Haven told me about a government regulation that stated if two close family members, such as a father and son or two brothers, were both in a combat zone, then one of the family members could volunteer to leave. He said he could get the paperwork I needed and suggested that I apply to leave Vietnam. He said his situation was much more secured than mine, and he would feel guilty if something were to happen to me. I told him I would think it over before deciding. I also argued that he had a wife at home and that I felt he should be the one to leave. The next day, Haven got me a hop on a small aircraft that took me back to my base camp. After arriving that afternoon, my unit headed back to our outpost (firebase), with constant shelling and harassment fire from "Charlie," a common nickname for Viet Cong or North Vietnam soldiers.

A couple of weeks after we spoke about one of us leaving Vietnam, I decided that if he didn't want to leave, I would. When it was my squad's time to make a supply run to base camp, I would go along and try to make contact with Haven. Once in base camp, where we had access to a special phone line, I was able to reach him. I told him to send the paperwork required to get out. He said he would start the process and send it to me for my signature. Within a couple of days, the paperwork was there, which I signed and sent back immediately.

Several days later, my platoon leader advised me that I would not be going on patrol that day but for me to get my gear as I would be going to base camp on the supply run later that day. He informed me I was leaving Vietnam as soon as they could issue my orders to leave. After a couple of days in base camp, my orders finally arrived. I was reassigned to Okinawa, Japan. That was not really what I had in mind, for I thought I would be going home. I left base camp on a helicopter heading to Tan Sun Nhut Air Force Base. Arriving there, I boarded a civilian airliner that was ready to leave immediately, so I only had a brief time with Haven before leaving. Goodbye, Vietnam!

It was late February 1970 when I arrived in Okinawa. Although it was nothing like being at home, I was comforted by the fact that the people there were not trying to kill us. My assignment in Okinawa was in a large warehouse where mechanics would repair any heavy or large equipment that arrived from Vietnam. Some of the equipment was not repairable. My specific job was to stock the warehouse; whenever our mechanics would request a particular part, I would pick them up from different warehouses. When I brought in parts, an invoice would accompany that part, which I would give to one of our clerks to file into inventory so we would know what parts we had in inventory and the location of each one.

All the clerks in our office were local Japanese citizens working for the US government. There were three females and three male clerks working in the office and one older gentleman working in the warehouse to deal with the Japanese mechanics when they needed parts. When I needed to discuss inventories with one of the clerks, I had a preference to one particular female clerk. Her name was Ritsuko Nagata. Usually, our conversations were strictly about business, but before long, we started having longer conversations that went beyond work. The other clerks in the office began to notice this.

At some point, I asked her out, but she refused, saying her grandmother would not allow her to date. More and more each day, we began to familiarize ourselves with each other through our conversations. Sometimes we shared our lunches. I continued to ask her out with continual rejections.

One day, I asked if she would like to go horseback riding at a stable that someone had told me about. To my surprise, she accepted my offer, thinking that I was an experienced rider. I had only ridden horses a couple of times in my life and had trouble each time I rode. I suppose my experience on the farm plowing with a mule and giving him voice commands did not work on a horse. I didn't realize a horse requires a pull on the reigns or a movement in the saddle to let him know what you want.

Ritsuko had never ridden a horse and was relying on my experience to help her. So much for that idea, but the strategy worked. We were now on a date away from work. Now I needed to give her other reasons that would convince her she made the right decision to go out with me. We left the stables and headed for a carnival on a nearby Air Force Base. I guess I impressed her enough that we would spend the next eight months dating and the next fifty years as husband and wife. We've had our ups and downs as other married couples have, but God has blessed us.

On February 1, 1971, I was discharged from the Army and decided to make our home in Naples, Florida, where my mother and younger brother were now living. My older sister had moved to Naples after finishing college. Naples was her husband's hometown. Since I had left Savannah at age seventeen, I had only gone back for short visits. I didn't have any strongholds there, even though my two sisters still lived in Savannah.

Naples, at that time, was a small Florida town on the Gulf of Mexico. The tropical climate there was almost a mirror to the climate Ritsuko was accustomed to in Okinawa. She was quick to fall in love with Naples. I landed my first job working for the US Geological Survey, which was mapping the Everglades. Ritsuko took a job at a local department store.

We worked continuously for the next two years, and in November 1972, Ritsuko gave birth to our first child. We decided to name her Andrea, a name that we really liked, and Yuki, a Japanese name that we both liked, Andrea Yuki Norris. We always called her Yuki. It was a full-term normal birth, but Yuki was born a very small baby, four pounds, and would be required to stay in the hospital until she was at least five pounds. Ritsuko was released after a couple of days, but Yuki took five weeks to gain the weight she needed before we could take her home. Not long after we took Yuki home, she developed episodes of having trouble breathing. She would turn blue, and we would rush her to the emergency room, where they would keep her for a few days.

After the second time in the emergency room, the doctor on call advised us that she appeared to have some major organ problems. They advised us to take her to the Children's Hospital in Miami for further testing. It was surprising that Yuki was almost two months old, and we were just hearing about major problems that should have been detected at her time of birth.

After a few weeks in Miami at the children's hospital, we were advised that Yuki was born with an extra chromosome, which caused some major organ problems. Her heart was turned at an improper angle, and her spleen had some major defects along with other medical deformities. The doctors in Miami had a positive outlook and said the heart could be corrected with surgery when she got older and gained weight.

We left Miami heartbroken, knowing that our only child would always be a special needs child and need medical attention for possibly many years to come. We would also need oxygen at home in case she needed it, as she often did. Her mislocated heart wasn't able to provide enough oxygenated blood to her body.

Back in Naples, we made several more trips to the emergency room with Yuki for fevers, low oxygen levels, and other problems. During one visit, a doctor at the hospital told us outright that our baby had so many problems that we should give her up now because she would not live long enough to have any surgery that could help her. We felt that was a cold way to talk to the parents of a child who was just beginning to coo and sometimes laugh; something we had not seen in the past. She was just beginning to follow her mom's movements when she laid her down and moved about her little crib. Now we were being told to let her go. Not on our lives!

When Yuki turned one, we decided to return to Okinawa to visit Ritsuko's parents. We wanted them to be near her and see their first grandchild. We left Naples and went to visit family in Georgia before going to Japan. We knew we would be gone for a year or more. After being in Georgia for a short time, Yuki became very ill and we had to admit her to the Brunswick hospital with pneumonia. She spent about a week in an oxygen tent to help with her breathing. She improved fairly fast, and after about a week, we were able to take her home. We were so very thankful for her speedy recovery, and we definitely gave thanks to God and for all who had been praying for her.

My older brother, Gerald, was involved with the Shriners Club in that area, and when he mentioned our situation to that group and that we were in transit to Japan, they very graciously picked up the cost for Yuki's hospital and doctors' fees. This was another blessing from God.

After the Brunswick incident, we decided to return to Naples and rethink our plans for Okinawa since we had already missed our flight schedule. While in Naples, we stayed at my sister's house for a few more weeks until we could make new travel arrangements. In January 1974, Helen and Brian drove us to Miami International Airport, where we would catch our flight to Okinawa. Although my mother had been very vocal about us going so far away and tried constantly to persuade us to change our minds, she understood our reasoning for Ritsuko's parents to have time with Yuki as well, and eventually gave us her blessings.

After arriving in Okinawa, I worked for Ritsuko's father in their laundry and dry-cleaning business. My job was to pick up and deliver laundry from the mostly Japanese population. It was fairly difficult not knowing the language very well since most of the customers were not fluent in English. Ritsuko helped me when her mother could watch Yuki. But most of the time, her mother was too busy with the business.

Things seemed to go good for Yuki until mid-March when Yuki got really sick with a high fever. We immediately took her to the local hospital, where they admitted her. They diagnosed her with pneumonia, then started her on antibiotics and other medications. We had her medical records from the US, but now we needed a Japanese doctor who could read English and understand her medical condition. Fortunately, the hospitals had a physician that had been educated in the US. We felt very good about the hospital's ability and were confident they would do everything they could to treat her.

Sadly, within a couple of days, we lost Yuki. It hit Ritsuko and me like an earthquake. We had been making plans to take her home with us within the next day or two. We were in the room with her when she started losing her color, so we called the nurse right away. The nurse checked her equipment and oxygen and realized a doctor was needed. The doctor was there immediately and started CPR while we watched helplessly. After working with her for a few minutes, the doctor had the nurse get an emergency kit that had a syringe loaded with a medication that was inserted into her chest to try and start the heart up again. After the injection, the doctor went back to chest compressions. This went on for several minutes until another doctor made the decision to halt the attempt to revive her. They had done all they could do for her, and we had witnessed their attempt. While the head doctor spoke with us, trying to comfort us, the doctor performing the CPR broke down sobbing. He tried not to let us see. We know he had done his best to revive her.

"*Suffer little children, and forbid them not to come unto me: for of such is the kingdom of heaven*" (Matt. 19:14).

Ritsuko was told at the hospital that if she had any particular clothes she wanted to dress Yuki in, she should do it right away. We called Ritsuko's mother at approximately one o'clock in the morning to break the sad news and ask her to bring the beautiful kimono Ritsuko's mother had recently purchased for her. When she arrived with the kimono, the nurses had already bathed her, and they helped dress her in her little kimono.

Not knowing the Japanese tradition, when they got her dressed, the nurse picked up her little body and put her in my arms, saying something in Japanese. She followed up with a bow of her head and tears in her eyes. Ritsuko explained that we now would take her home with us. Traditionally, the Japanese would send the body home until the next day in which they would cremate and have a funeral. What would I do at this point? I thought they would take her to a morgue or somewhere until a funeral could be planned. We arrived home around two am.

I needed some help in my thinking about what to do, so I called a cousin, William Norris, who worked for the US government in Okinawa for about thirty years. I woke him up in the wee hours of the morning, giving him our sad news about Yuki. We told him that we had her body at home with us. He expressed his sympathies and said he would make a few phone calls and then call me back. After a short time, he called back, saying he had called the military mortician and woke him up to explain our situation. He advised us to get as much ice as possible on her to keep her body cool until he could get the okay from others to allow us to use the Army mortuary. Sometime after eight o'clock in the morning, he called us with the directions to the Army mortuary and said he would meet us there to take possession of Yuki's body. I have not mentioned that this was a Sunday morning, and no one would normally be working there. Thank God he was willing to do this for us. He would put her in a refrigerated vault where we would now have time to decide what we wanted to do.

We called my mom before we went to the mortuary to let her know about Yuki and asked that she let everyone else know. Sometime that day, we received a call from the pastor of the Naples Church of God, Reverend Walter Lauster. He called to offer his sympathy, encourage us, and prayed for us over the phone. That was really touching.

On Monday, we had a call from someone that could authorize us to use the military mortuary. I think my cousin pulled some strings with people he knew to get us that approval in a short period of time. This allowed the mortician to prep Yuki and have her body shipped back to the US for burial.

Within a couple of days, we had a small funeral in the mortuary chapel attended by family and a few people from the local Church of God who sang a few songs. The service was short. The next day, the Army took charge to fly her remains back to Georgia, where my mother, along with others, had planned and arranged a funeral in Jesup, Georgia. My mom, sister, and family had driven up from Naples to make arrangements for the funeral. I have to give thanks to everyone for his or her prayers and attendance at the service.

"The Lord is my shepherd: I shall not want. He maketh me to lie down in green pastures: He leadeth me beside the still waters. He restoreth my soul: He leadeth me in the paths of righteousness for his names sake. Yea though I walk through the valley of the shadow of death, I will fear no evil: for thou art with me; Thy rod and Thy staff they comfort me. Thou prepares a table before me in the presence of mine enemies: Thou annointest my head with oil; my cup runneth over. Surely goodness and mercy shall follow me all the days of my life; and I will dwell in the house of the Lord forever" (**Ps. 23:1–6**).

We continued living in Okinawa and grieving like any other parent who had lost a child. In early March, one year later, Ritsuko gave birth to our son Rick. As expected, parents would have great concerns after losing one child from birth defects. However, Rick was born a healthy baby with normal weight, and we gave praise to God for him.

We spent the next six months trying to decide whether to stay in Okinawa or come back to the US. I was rather homesick myself and wanted to leave, but I knew it would be hard on Ritsuko. Finally, we decided to leave Okinawa and return to the US. We landed in Jesup, Georgia. We lived there about ten months before deciding to move back to Naples, Florida, where we lived prior to going to Okinawa.

Once settled in Naples, I left Ritsuko and Rick living with my mom. Mom had finished school and was a licensed practical nurse. She had opened a private nursing care facility, and Ritsuko was working there, helping her.

I was in Homestead, Florida, for about six weeks, getting trained as a heavy equipment operator and coming home on the weekends. After finishing my training, I returned to Naples to start my career as a heavy equipment operator. That lasted about three months before I realized there was more money to be made as a union labor at that time.

I worked in construction for about a year when an old friend surveyor called and asked if I wanted to get into surveying. After agreeing, I did what I loved most, working in the woods, where I felt most comfortable. In 1988, I was granted my certification for Professional Land Surveyor and Mapper. I continued working as a surveyor and eventually opened my own surveying company.

For the next twenty years, I surveyed until my health began to fail as a result of exposure to Agent Orange while I was in Vietnam. In 1997, I was diagnosed with type two diabetes. Additionally, in 2008, I began suffering from kidney failure. Then in January 2011, after having chest pains, I was told that I needed a triple heart bypass.

During surgery, my doctor determined that one of the blockages was in an area that was too difficult to get to, so he decided to just do a double bypass instead. The doctor also indicated the one blockage would possibly find a new route for the blood to flow to get to where it was needed. Then, in May 2019, I had a pacemaker implanted.

I consider all the things I've been through, miracle after miracle. Through all this, I am still blessed with my beautiful wife and son Rick, who have been by my side all along.

Rick and Vickie Norris

Gloria Norris Adams

As told by Gloria Adams to Brian Johnson

Stan, Gloria's husband, came from a strong Christian family, and his parents left a faith heritage to their children and grandchildren: Stanley Jr., Jason, and Jamie. Gloria is the youngest daughter of Joel Allen Norris Sr. and Beatrice Cobb Norris.

Gloria and Stan Adams

Gloria had married Stanley Adams and was beginning her life as a young wife. She and Stan were living in Jesup, Georgia, when Gloria decided to seek employment at a radio station, thinking she might like to work as a DJ. Uncle Marshall's radio program was aired on Sundays on WLOP in Jesup, which primarily played country music during the week. Naturally, on Sundays, they would have faith-based programming as families prepared for church. The station manager offered

Gloria a job, but she turned them down because of the type of music they played.

In 1974, she began working for WSOJ (**W**onderful **S**ounds **O**f Joy), a Christian radio station in Jesup, Georgia. While working in Jesup, she would visit "all-night singings," gospel singing concerts, which would often last from sundown to sunup. She interviewed and had conversations with the singers and broadcast that information over the air for the listening audience in the days following the concerts. Gloria worked there until she and Stan moved back to Savannah in 1976. During that time, she interviewed with the Dee Rivers Group. Before her interview, she asked Uncle Marshall to pray for her that she would pass the interview. He prayed for her, and she landed the job!

Gloria Sitting at the Radio Console

The Rivers Group is a company that presently has several stations in the Southeast Georgia area. This group of stations was owned by the former governor of Georgia, E. D. Rivers, and was managed by his son. When E. D. passed away, he left the group of stations to his grandchildren. Gloria also worked a number of years for Cumulous Adventure Radio. She later returned to the Rivers Group and is now an officer in the corporation. She progressed from DJ to management, then found herself promoted to a director, a position she still holds to this day.

Gloria recently commented, "I have been blessed to spread the gospel through radio since 1974. I love the medium of radio."

Because of her involvement in radio, Gloria was able to assist her sister, Julia, in obtaining a radio license for the radio station she and her church own and operate in Bloomingdale, Georgia. Spread the good news of salvation! We will tell!

"One generation shall praise thy works to another, and shall declare thy mighty acts. I will speak of the glorious honour of thy majesty, and of thy wondrous works" (**Ps. 145:4–5**).

What a legacy we have inherited because of our parents, grandparents, and great grandparents!

Philip Randall Norris Sr.

As told by: Helen Johnson

Philip Randall Norris is the youngest child born to Joel and Beatrice Norris. He is the father of Katie, Joseph, Philip Jr., and Sarah. He has one grandson, Joseph. Philip lives in Twin Cities, Georgia.

In 1960, I was five years old. While in the backyard on Anderson Street, where my daddy was working, I caught two of my fingers in the saw blade. Daddy always carried his anointing oil with him wherever he went. He anointed me with oil, prayed for me, and took me to the hospital for stiches. The doctor looked at the injury and told Daddy one of the fingers could not be saved and asked if Daddy wanted him to take the finger off. I said, "No."

They left both fingers intact to heal. The decision was made to take skin from one of my legs and graft it to my emaciated finger, leaving a very unsightly scar for the rest of my life. The scar always reminds me of God's grace.

Philip Norris Jr.

One of the saddest days of my life in 2012, my son Joseph was killed in an automobile accident while returning home from work. He loved life, God, and the Word. He was such a caring young man. During the last hours of his grandmother's life, he held her hand and read Scripture to her. He left a legacy, having been taught God's Word.

Joseph Norris

"When I call to remembrance the unfeigned faith that is in thee, which dwelt first in thy grandmother Lois and my mother Eunice ..." (2 Tim. 1:5).

The Anderson Family

Linh Hopkins

*L*inh Hopkins is the first-born child to Haven Parker Anderson. *She has one younger step-brother, Haven Jr. They are the grandchildren of Clayton and Annie Anderson. Clayton was a lay minister at Stoney Hill Baptist Church. Linh and her husband Jim Hopkins live in Champaign, Illinois, where she owns her own business. They have three children, Jordin, Hope, and Payton.*

"I am your Creator. You were in my care even before you were born" (Isa. 44:2a CEV).

Linh Hopkins, daughter of Haven Parker Anderson Sr.

In 1967, when my mom was twenty-two years old, she met an American Air Force officer in Saigon, and the two fell in love. He was very attentive to her and cared for her deeply. Their relationship grew and matured. He wanted to marry her, but her family didn't give her permission to do so. Her family had feared their relationship would be discovered, and marrying an American soldier could risk the family getting killed. My sister, Minh, became a result of that loving relationship. His tour serving in Vietnam soon ended, and he had to return to the United States.

Haven P. Anderson Sr. at 17 Joins the Air Force

Sometime in 1969, my mother met my father. He was also in the United States Air Force. Mom was twenty-four years old when they met. She was working as a housekeeper in Saigon. He saw my mother and fell in love. They had a sweet loving relationship. My father adored my sister, who was a toddler at the time. They lived and shared an apartment together during his time in Vietnam. He would come and go during his service time there. He and Mom did have a language barrier between them, but they managed. He was well liked by many in the neighborhood.

Sometime in late summer 1970, my father left Vietnam to go back to the US. After my father left, my mother realized she was pregnant with me. Before the war ended, my father came back to Vietnam to where they once shared a home looking for my mother, but she had relocated. They never reunited again, nor did he get the opportunity to learn that he had a daughter. My mother was heartbroken and never spoke of him much. It was painful for her to talk about him, and so, for that reason, she always said to leave it alone every time I would ask questions about my father.

When Saigon fell to the Communists in 1975, I was four years old. I remember standing in the street, holding my mother's hand as we watched the Vietnamese Communist soldiers marching through our city, waving their flags accompanied by military tanks. I saw my mother cry along with many other Vietnamese people. At the age of four, I did not understand much of what was going on, but I knew it was sad for my mother.

My mother, along with many Southern Vietnamese people, had to hide any hints or evidence that they were involved with the enemy, the American soldiers. She burned everything that belonged to my father that he left behind, including any documentation pertaining to my father's personal information and photos.

I remember my mother sat us down and explained to us what was going on in our country. She warned us not to say too much, and we needed to watch how we acted. "Do not let anyone know what we have in our home."

We could not even reveal how much food we had for fear that the Vietcong would come for us and take all of what we had. My mother believed that impending Communist rule would not serve us well during our life in Vietnam. There would be no property rights, no individual freedom, and everybody would be under constant suspicion should citizens even be suspected of veering from the Communist Party line.

Mom knew her daughters would not have freedom if we stayed in Vietnam. We were terribly mistreated by the people because we were biracial. We endured the racism from the people that hated the way we looked because our fathers were Americans. We were the product of the war, and therefore, the children of the enemy.

The people looked down on my mother. The mistreatment also came from my mother's own family as they shunned her for having "mixed" children. In turn, we also endured my mother's relentless stress, which she often took out on us. We were often told to go back to where we came from. My mother knew when my sister turned sixteen years of age, she would be drafted to serve in the military for the Vietcong. She wanted us to experience the freedom from our fathers' land. My mother knew that she had to do everything within her power to find a way out of Vietnam for both of her daughters.

Our journey to the United States began on November 22, 1981, in Saigon. I was ten years old, and my sister Minh was thirteen when we set out to escape Vietnam. Mom sent us off to meet a gentleman who would be our guide for the journey. He brought us as far as where we needed to be. We then met up with others who also had planned to escape. We didn't know anyone. We walked many nights through rice fields and the jungle. We then boarded a boat that was packed with 141 passengers.

Minh and I got separated on the boat early on. We sat apart from each other. Clearly, this boat was designed to comfortably accommodate maybe twenty or thirty people. There was no space to easily walk from one part of the boat to another. There were just too many people.

First night out at sea, we were hit by a massive storm. We lost all our food and water supplies. We also lost our one and only captain in the storm. We floated in the ocean for ten days without food and fresh water. I had no concept of time or day of the week. I was sandwiched in by strangers around me, crammed on the lower level of the boat. Some adults yelled me at because I got seasick and threw up. They did not know whom I belonged to. No adult claimed me, and the only relative I had with me was my thirteen-year-old sister somewhere on the same boat.

Hours turned into days as we drifted. I remember looking around as far as my eyes could see. I saw sadness. I saw tears. I saw fear. Nighttime was peaceful as we floated, and people slept. I lost track of time and didn't know how many days had passed since Minh and I were separated. Then, there was a short window of time and space for me to move about in search for Minh. When I finally found her, she didn't look well. I thought for sure she was dying. I managed to get my hands on a can of condensed milk. There wasn't much left in it. I tried to feed Minh with it. I once again got yelled at. There were the same questions, "Who is this kid? Whom does she belong to?"

Perhaps I got yelled at because I took the condensed milk or no one knew who I was after days at sea. Perhaps the energy that was left in me didn't sink in that we all were slowly dying. We were tired, hungry, and thirsty. Slowly, kids died around us. The same children that I had sat and played with earlier were now dying. Ultimately twenty-nine people perished from starvation and dehydration. Twenty-seven of them were children. My sister and I were the two youngest children that survived. On our tenth day adrift on the unforgiving waters, we were rescued and towed to shore by Thai fishermen. The 112 survivors were placed in refugee camps in Thailand.

The refugee camps we stayed in were all similar to each other. Wires and metal fences kept people in surrounded camps. There were many buildings that looked the same. We were given small portions of water and food each day. Generally, the "meal" was soup broth, rice, and one piece of meat.

I remember the camp would sound off the siren to welcome another group of refugees to the camp. We would run as close as we could to the gate to see if any of those new refugees included our mom. In my mind, I was hoping maybe she had changed her mind and decided to take the same journey and join us. We would repeat the rush to the gate each and every time the siren would sound off. The weeks turned into months. My sister and I always ran to the gate but never saw Mom stepping off one of those busses that transported new refugees. As time passed, so did my little wishful mind's hope of seeing Mom. We moved around and stayed in three different refugee camps for eighteen months before we were granted proper documentation to go to the United States of America.

We arrived in the US in June 1983. My sister and I were placed in a foster home together. In the early years of growing up in the US, there were many blessings and challenges. I struggled with learning the language and keeping up with school. I had to learn and adapt to the new culture.

I started attending school in seventh grade. I didn't have any friends, and I was so scared. Every day at school, I just kept to myself, as this was what I was used to doing most of my life. I was often locked up alone for most of my young life in Vietnam while Mom had to go to work. My only view of the outside world was from a secured second-floor balcony of our home. I would watch the children play outside on the street and often wished I was one of them. I spent most of my days gazing outside and daydreaming. I missed out on the crucial age of social interaction.

The first few months of school in the US were exceedingly difficult for me. Every day at lunchtime, I would hide under the school stairwell and refuse to go into the cafeteria to eat. I just didn't know what to do. Who would I sit with? How would I talk if I couldn't understand the language? How would I fit in? It was scary and quite traumatic for me.

I kept most of my struggles to myself. I didn't think anyone could understand what I was going through. I didn't know how to share this with my foster parents. I didn't know English well enough to share. Even if I did speak English well, I didn't want to be any trouble for them. I was worried that had I shared my struggles, they may have thought I didn't like them or their home wasn't good enough, and for that, I would be sent away to somewhere else.

After less than three years of living at my foster parents' home, my sister, who had been my primary caregiver since an incredibly young age, left for college three hours away. I didn't have a full understanding of college and the American school system. I had to deal with another change in my life. I felt as if I had lost another mother. One more thing was taken away from me. The sense of abandonment overcame me once again.

One scared and confused child was who I was for most of my young life. I was so sad that Mom was not with us on our journey escaping Vietnam. We waited for her in the refugee camps for so many months, and she didn't show up. During my teen years, I had so many questions about my life and the circumstances in front of me. I was angry that Mom let us go. I thought perhaps by letting us go, life would be easier on Mom, and she didn't have to deal with us anymore.

I had many questions about my father. Who was he? What was his name? What did he look like? And why did Mom not want to talk about him? I needed to understand my heritage. I didn't really know Mom well either. Sure, I have her pictures, but I really didn't know her as a person. Many of these questions that may seem insignificant to some people are especially important to me. It is difficult when you go through life not knowing half of your genetic makeup. As time passed, I grew up and got busy with life. I set my desire to search for my father aside.

Linh Hopkins Family: Jordin, Peyton, Linh, Jim, and Hope

In 1993, I met my husband. We have three beautiful children. My husband is a godly man, and I am so thankful for him. I have always believed in God and the power of something that is so much bigger than I can wrap my mind around. However, prior to meeting my husband, I was not attending church regularly.

We found a church that we love and became members. We were married in our church. My faith grew stronger as I studied God's Word. I was determined to get to know Christ in a much deeper level. I wanted to have a personal relationship with him. The more I studied His Word, the more I was eager to learn more. I needed to understand my purpose in this life and why I was spared so many times in my life. I read as many Christian books as my time was allowed in between operating my businesses and running after three small children. I decided to fast for two weeks while I dived into God's words. It was not easy to fast, not eating at all for two weeks, but I felt empowered to try. I figured if Jesus could do it for forty days, I surely could do it for fourteen days.

"Never will I leave you; never will I forsake you" (**Heb. 13:5b NIV**).

One of the books that spoke right into my heart was *The Purpose Driven Life*, by Rick Warren, which seemed to be written specifically for me:

> You are not an accident. Your birth was no mistake or mishap, and your life is no fluke of nature. Your parents may not have planned you, but God did. He was not at all surprised by your birth. In fact, he expected it. Long before your parents conceived you, you were conceived in the mind of God. He thought of you first. It is not fate, nor chance, nor luck, nor coincidence that you are breathing at this very moment. You are alive because God wanted to create you!

I needed to hear those words. I felt reaffirmed that I should never feel ashamed for not knowing my birth father. I can answer with joy and confidence when people ask what I am mixed with. It settles in my childhood memory of being haunted with the question, "Who is this kid, and who does she belong to?" The stigma of who I am and how I came about is no longer that thorn in my side. I am a child of God. That is who I am. He wanted me, and He has a plan for my life. He is my heavenly Father, and He has been walking beside me my whole life.

Joy and love poured over me when I accepted Christ to be my Lord and Savior. God unveiled and allowed me to understand all of my childhood fear, struggles, and sadness. I finally understood the sacrifice my mother had to make to give us a better life by sending us away to the land of my father. I understood that Mom didn't lock me up because she was mean or cruel. She did it to keep me safe from being kidnapped while she had to work to put food on the table. She did the absolute best she knew how. Many biracial children like us were discarded, abandoned, and worse yet, they were kidnapped and sold. Mom could have discarded us like many other mothers with Amerasian children. But Mom decided to keep us for as long as she could in a country with people who were cruel to us, even after being shunned by her own family.

I understand the unwavering love my foster parents had shown us, even though we are not their own. Their compassion and godly love for us was immeasurable. We needed a home, and we needed parents. They were there to love and support us. They took a chance on us, even though they did not know our inner struggles. But they were steadfast in their compassion and commitment to foster us.

God sent us angels along the way when we needed them. Our foster parents are among those angels. God kept us safe and helped us survive the ocean while so many people died around us. This simply was not by chance or luck. God was there with us, and He knew our time on this earth was not up yet. I have personally been spared so many times in my life that I have no doubt I have God's favor.

"For by grace you have been saved through faith, and that not of yourselves; it is the gift of God" (Eph. 2:8).

In fall 2016, with the encouragement of my children, I purchased a DNA test kit. They knew how curious I have been about my genetic makeup. At first, I had no interest because I didn't understand anything about it. After more persuasion, I gave in and bought the test kit. The kit came, and I followed the instructions on how to do it. I then sent the test back and waited for the results. It took about six weeks for my results to come back. I was so excited, nervous, and curious as to what my heritage was.

I've been fascinated by what I have learned with my DNA results. I was surprised to also receive a list of DNA matches of distant relatives from my father's side of the family. The closest DNA relative I had on the list was a second cousin. I sat with that information for a while and didn't know what to do. I prayed prior to making the decision to pursue my search. I have thought often as to what I would do if I had the opportunity to find my father. I was cautious about what I may find and what I would do if I were to face the possibility of meeting him. Would I even want to do that? Would I disrupt his family dynamics? Ultimately, I decided that all I wanted was his name, but if I were blessed to have a picture, it would be amazing, and whatever happened after that would be in God's will.

With my son's help, it took us seven months on and off to do my research. Then, we got stuck and unable to move forward with the search on our own. I decided to reach out to a professional genealogist. She was happy to assist us. She asked permission to take over my research and got going with it. It took her only two weeks to give me the results of her search. She reached back out to me and gave me information about the family line and my father's name. She also gave me two names and advised me to reach out to them for concrete confirmation. One of the names was my half-brother, Haven Jr. I prayed prior to reaching out and sending him a message.

I tried to be thoughtful and careful how I approached him with the message. I wanted to be certain and careful to not assume and assert that his father was my biological father. I also did not want to come across that I posed any harm or ill will. I just needed confirmation about my potential biological father.

I was nervous and a bit hesitant as I hit the "send" button to contact my brother. I didn't expect a response right away. The DNA results could have been totally wrong. Or my newly discovered family member may have had zero interest and be completely annoyed with my contact. Or the DNA results could be correct. However, seconds after I hit "send," my brother responded. He was open and willing to help. Not only did he confirm my father's name but he also sent a picture of my father along with a picture of my father's headstone. It was so surreal as I sat there and stared at the photograph of my father. I was so happy! Not only did I get confirmation of his name but I also got a picture of him. I was so in awe that it didn't register to me in the moment that he had passed away many years ago. I was just so thrilled with the name. After that moment, I almost logged off the computer to just disappear as if I were never there.

Ronald, Philip Bea, and Gerald at Haven's Funeral

Before I knew it, my brother naturally and rightfully wanted to know more information about me. I paused and thought to myself, "What a jerk would I be if I just disappeared and failed to respond." I talked myself through the process and simply told myself to be brave. He wanted a picture of me. I sent the most recent one I had. He responded that he saw our resemblance and said that if I were not his sister, he would be shocked. I did not see what he saw right away. My father's face was new to me. I didn't get a chance to really study it and compare the features yet.

What happened next was sweet. He gave me his phone number and said he would love to talk more about our family discovery if I called him. So, I did! And the way he answered the phone was so exceedingly kind. He answered by saying, "What's up, sis?" He did not hesitate to call me "sis," and we had just made connection only about twenty minutes earlier. Our conversation did not last long as he was on his way to work that day.

The next day, my brother messaged, telling me that he had spoken with one of the uncles, and the uncle confirmed that my father did have a lady friend in Vietnam, and he remembered meeting my mom. My brother wanted to know if there was anything he needed to do. I told him that there wasn't anything he was obligated to do. But if he would like to be certain that we are siblings, I would be happy to send him a DNA test kit for him to take. My brother agreed, and so I sent a test kit to him. It did not take long for the results to come back, and the test confirmed us to be siblings.

I shared the good news with my sister right away, and she was so happy and incredibly supportive, as were my parents. However, it took me a few weeks to process my newly found family before I was able to share the news with my biological mother. My biological mother had been living in the US since 1999. My sister and I decided to sponsor and bring our mother to the US to be near her grandchildren and us. I did not know how she would handle the news. I didn't know if she would be upset, mad, or sad. She had told me many times not to talk about my father, ask too many questions, and simply let it go. I prayed for God to guide my words and me as I shared the news with my biological mother.

On a beautiful sunny afternoon, I got off work early. I came home, and I stood in the front room of my home. I had not even taken my purse off my shoulder yet. I felt a nudge in my gut, telling me to be brave and go to Mom's house and share the news with her. The short drive to her house seemed forever long. I got to Mom's house, and she was in the backyard tending to her garden. We chatted for a bit about my daughter Hope being away at Fort Jackson in basic training with the military. It was my window of opportunity to talk about military and my father. The conversation about my father did not happen, but here we were; it was now or never. I went for it!

With my now limited Vietnamese vocabulary, I told her I found my father's side of the family by doing DNA testing. The look on her face was pure confusion to say the least. I explained how it was done. She asked if I was certain with the information that I had received. At this point, we were still waiting for the DNA test result from my brother to come back to confirm for certain. But I told her that he had sent me a photo of my father and asked if she would like to see it. Her hands were shaking as she grabbed the phone from my hands. She quietly nodded her head and said, "That's him. I have not seen this face in so many years."

The tears rolled down her cheeks, and she wanted to sit down. We sat on the back step of her house for a while in silence. I think she needed time to process it. She then asked me to come inside and wait for her. She went into her bedroom and came out with two handkerchiefs. She handed them to me and said "You can have them now. These belonged to your father. He left them behind, and I could not bring myself to get rid of them when the Communists came in, even though I had to burn everything else that belonged to him so we wouldn't get in trouble with the Communists."

I was completely surprised that she held onto something that belonged to my father for forty-six years and never said a thing to me. During the moment, I didn't want to bother her with many questions and make her relive her pain and sadness. It is her story, and I must respect it. I treasure whatever bits and pieces of memories she has of my father whenever she is comfortable and willing to share.

I got a voicemail from my Aunt Helen with her sweet Southern accent; she introduced herself as my father's younger sister. She wanted to meet me and invited us to her home in Tennessee. During Labor Day weekend 2017, my son and I took the adventure to Cleveland, Tennessee, to meet Aunt Helen, her husband Brian, and their family.

My husband, Jim, and my oldest daughter, Jordin, were busy and unable to go. My second daughter was at Fort Jackson in basic training with the US Army. My son, Payton, was my moral support buddy for the weekend. It was a long eight-hour drive through the beautiful mountains of Tennessee.

I was nervous as I rang the doorbell to my aunt's home. She opened the door with a welcoming smile. In her hand, she held a large piece of paper with my picture printed out. I think she wanted to make sure I looked the same as I claimed on the Internet. We spent the first evening getting to know each other.

The next morning, Aunt Helen, her husband, my son, and I drove about five hours to Glennville, Georgia to visit my father's gravesite. I wanted to pay my respect to him as soon as I knew he wasn't alive. When we arrived at the cemetery, it was amazing to see there were other family members there to meet us. I was so honored they made an effort to meet my son and me.

There were so many thoughts running through my mind at my father's grave. Many mixed emotions consumed me. I saw all the names on the headstones that I recognized from my seven months of researching and building the family tree that helped find my father. All the names that I had stared at and studied for so long were now in front of me as I walked through the cemetery. I felt as if I knew them all. The unknown world of the other half of my identity for forty-six years was now all in front of me. There are no words to describe how joy-filled and happy I was!

After the cemetery visit, we went to a restaurant before we headed back to Tennessee. It was lovely, and I was at a loss for words while I was eating and trying to keep my emotions in check. Where should I even begin? How does someone catch up after forty-six years? What questions should I ask, and whom should I ask? Listening is what I do best. Thus, I allowed the moment that felt so surreal to play out.

At the end of May 2019, we took another memorable trip to Naples, Florida, to meet two more uncles, Uncle Ronnie, his wife Ritsuko, and Uncle Phillip. We had a wonderful time. They both were kind, very welcoming, and loving. They shared with me some information about my father, stories about themselves and the family, and then we looked through old photos. The visit was lovely, and they were very hospitable.

"Blessed are those who mourn, for they shall be comforted" (Matt. 5:4).

For the first three years after finding the family, I underwent many ups and downs emotionally. It was difficult trying to figure out how to fit in. I went through the joy of finding my father and learning of his name. When I finally learned his name and saw his photo for the first time, the excitement of it was so amazing that it didn't register with me right away that he had passed.

When I had time to process my father's death, I then felt angry. I was not angry with anyone in particular. I was angry at life's circumstances and wished I could have had the chance to meet him. But I was too late. I relied on my faith, and through many prayers, I finally was able to grieve. I grieved for a man I did not know and a lifetime of questions that would remain unanswered. God knew I couldn't have handled it any sooner.

God's timing is perfect, and I trust His plan for this journey of finding my father was exactly how it was meant to be. I shared my emotions with Aunt Helen, who comforted me with her kind words, "...I know your grandmother is dancing with joy in heaven knowing about you ...and someday we will rejoice in heaven, and you will receive a hug only a father could give." How blessed am I to have such godly people in my life!

I had put off taking the trip to meet my brother in California. There were many different reasons why I could not make the trip a lot sooner. We are an active family with busy schedules. The three kids were busy with schools, jobs, and military commitments that it was difficult to find time when we all could travel together as a family. My wish was for us to experience meeting my brother together as a family. Besides the hectic, busy schedules, my father and my sister had their medical scares. I didn't feel it was the right time to travel. I was worried about being far away from home. On top of that, we had to endure the COVID-19 pandemic for another year, which further delayed traveling. I was extremely reluctant to travel and risk getting sick.

In February 2021, I was blessed with a lovely birthday celebration with my family. The kids gave me a wonderful surprise gift. The gift was a trip to meet my brother! They had made all the arrangements for my husband and my son to join me. What a thoughtful and generous gift!

On April 30, 2021, my brother and I finally met in person. He gave me the biggest hug. He was sweet and very welcoming. Our visit with my brother and his family was wonderful. We didn't really discuss very much about our pasts. I shared a bit more about my journey escaping from Vietnam, but we mainly just enjoyed getting to know each other. We spent two days visiting and remaining present. Certainly, I wish we had more time, but we needed to get back home.

Haven, Linh, and Haven Anderson III–Initial Meeting

I received a kind and heartfelt message from my brother after we said our goodbyes. "Just so you know, this weekend meant the world to me. You and your family are amazing. I am truly honored to be your favorite little brother. I know, in my heart, our dad is just so proud of his little girl. Safe travels, and God bless."

How blessed am I to have had this experience! I know from meeting my brother that I am certain our father would be just as proud of his son. I truly am humbled and honored to have met my little brother.

"*Before I formed you in the womb, I knew you. Before you were born, I set you apart*" (Jer. 1:5 NIV).

As I reflect on my life, there was trauma, many difficulties, and sadness, but I was also blessed with many joyful events. Early on as young children, my sister and I struggled with our biracial identity, and we were not accepted by the Vietnamese culture. The value of our journey, escaping our birth country, and leaving our mother for a chance at a better life is incalculable.

Our experience living in refugee camps taught us courage and independence. Our struggles in learning a new language and a different culture influenced us to who we are today. Through my daily walks with God as I continue to study His Word, I understand and see the fabrics of our lives, which have been woven by God's amazing work.

He had put the right people in our lives to guide and love us along the way. Our wonderful parents, Andrew and Dolores, are the prime example. We have such gratitude and deep love for them. They were my rock and the stability that I needed during my vulnerable years.

I'm also blessed to have my biological mother here with us in the United States; the gift of opportunity to get to know her and make up for the many years we lost. I admire my mom's courage and strength for the sacrifices she had to make so we could have a better life. I surely love and respect her tremendously.

I now have my father's side of the family, who is kind and accepting. It is a gift to learn that my father's family is strong in their walk with God, and they are prayerful and faithful people. Where we are today is not short of miracles. The joys I experience are from the grace and miracles I feel each day. I am blessed to be healthy and alive. As God's child, I understand where I belong—in Him.

One of my many favorite verses, which I strive to live by each day, is Psalm 46:10: "Be still and know that I am God." This verse continues to give me strength and keep me grounded when I need it the most. I have been reminded many times throughout my life that just how much of this life I will never fully understand. Only God can see from the beginning to the end. I hold onto God's promise and humble myself to be still enough to let Him be the guide of my life. I have entrusted my life to Him to bring Him the glory. I treasure the mercy He has given to me when I fall short. His abundant blessings have showered upon me to show me that I am truly blessed!

"So be strong and courageous! Do not be afraid and do not panic before them. For the Lord, your God will personally go ahead of you. He will neither fail you nor abandon you" (Deut. 31:6 NLP).

Minh Aimone

Minh Aimone is an Amerasian woman, who, at age thirteen, immigrated to the United States from Vietnam along with her younger sister Linh, who was later discovered to be the daughter of Haven Parker Anderson. During their journey, she and her sister were placed in refugee camps and moved from Thailand to Hong Kong to Los Angeles and to Chicago. They eventually settled in a foster home in Champaign, Illinois. She works at Gies College of Business as an office support staff. She became involved with Amerasians Without Borders, a non-profit organization that helps Amerasians in Vietnam come to the US. She and her three children live in Champaign, Illinois.

Minh Aimone – Linh's Sister

In the last thirty-eight years living in the US, the common questions that I've been asked include "Where are you from?"; "Where are you really from?"; "Where is that accent from?"; "How did you get here?"; "Aren't Vietnamese people Buddhists?"; "What was it like when you found God?"; and "What is it like to have a family with three different faiths?" Although they are harmless questions and with no ill intention, asked only out of curiosity, they often trigger various thoughts and emotions at different seasons of my life and serve as reminders of my journey in search for identity, roots, belonging, and acceptance.

When I reflect on the life journey and lessons I learned along the way, from childhood to adolescence, emerging adulthood, and now way into my middle-aged season of life, I'm in awe of how God has worked meticulously in my earthly and spiritual life. Everything was meant to be, and everything was and is in God's timing. His words have taught me time and again what it means to lean on God and be patient with His timing.

We often want things from God, and we do forget that we're expecting things to happen in our own earthly timing and understanding. That's never the case with God. His timing for each one of us, when we experience trying, growing times, and when we mature enough, is to share, teach, and serve in His glorious name.

Friends and acquaintances wonder what it is like living in a family with three different faiths. Some also have made assumptions by considering where I was born that I should have been practicing the Buddhist faith and not the Christian faith. I'd say that God works in mysterious ways, and if we don't pay attention, we may miss an opportunity to learn powerful lessons. Things are not always what they seem, and we never know how God has worked in someone's life or what journey he or she has traveled to arrive where he or she is today.

I was born to a mother who practiced Buddhism, and I was fostered by American parents who practice Roman Catholicism, who were and still are active in their church. I decided to follow Jesus by studying the Bible because I made a decision that if and when I became a parent, I wanted my children to have a foundation. One may ask, "But how and what led you to that decision?" The answers take me back to my childhood.

One day while hanging out with my elementary school friends when I was still in Vietnam, around the ages of ten to eleven, I was introduced to or heard of Jesus's name for the very first time. My friends were

Catholic, and the church they attended was within walking distance of our school. The church was open to the public for anyone to come in and pray throughout the day.

My friends were going to pray and asked if I would come along, and I came along, not to pray but just to be with my friends. I knelt next to them and was very puzzled by the entire ordeal and experience. My eyes, of course, were fixed on the figure hanging on the cross before me above the stage. It looked scary to me. He hardly had any clothes on, just a cloth, a thorny ring on his head, and blood on his side.

I couldn't understand why my friends were worshiping this figure in front of them. I asked who that was and why He was up there. They replied that it was Jesus, and He died for our sins. I responded that I did not have any sins. I did a mental check quietly to myself, "Have I sinned? Was lying to my mother now and then why I was coming home late from school a sin?"

But more than questioning my own sins, I compared notes to what sins meant based on my mother's teachings. From her teaching, there was no one to die for my sins. If I were to sin, I'd go straight to hell, and there was a specific punishment for each sin according to hell's law. And I had no idea where she learned that. All I know is that it was so scary that I tried not to sin.

My mother was a member of one of the large Buddhist temples in a nearby town. We had to travel there by bus. The Buddhist temple held ceremony feasts on the first and fifteenth of the month. She took my sister and me there on a regular basis, and we learned various chants that we were expected to memorize.

When I came home, I asked my mother about Jesus because I wanted to know if what my friends said was true. What my mother told me about Jesus was nothing like what my friends said. I was told not to ask again about Him.

At another time, I asked my friends about Him again and was told that Jesus was the Son of God. I questioned why God let His Son die like that, the thoughts going through my head and childish mind. It bothered me, and I was determined to find out the truth, once and for all. I didn't know what I didn't know. I didn't know if truth was not told or none of them knew who that man was on the cross. I had the feeling that something was very important about that Jesus. Otherwise, they wouldn't put Him in a church. I was told that church was a holy place similar to the temple my mother took me to. Jesus was on my mind since that day.

"The Lord is my shepherd" (*Ps. 23:1*).

That was the beginning of my quest to know Jesus.

Being an Amerasian child in Vietnam and under the Communist regime, life was brutal and grim. My sister and I were bullied by neighborhood and school kids for the way we looked. We soon learned we were biracial and that we looked different than other kids. We just couldn't understand why we kept being told to go back to our country. Vietnam was *our* country; it was where we were born. But we soon realized "our country" meant America because our fathers were Americans. Of course, I went to my mother for answers, and she did her best to explain. Little did I know around that age what *My Lai* was. *My Lai* in Vietnamese means Amerasian.

What is an Amerasian? Vietnamese Amerasians are children of American servicemen or American contractors and Vietnamese women during the Vietnam War. It was estimated that there were over 50,000 to 70,000 and as many as 100,000 Amerasians born during the Vietnam War between the years 1965 and 1975.

When my sister and I left Vietnam, we didn't fully understand what Amerasian was. In fact, we never heard of the word until we were in our foster parents' home. The social worker and our foster mom told us what we were. We never met another Amerasian until 2007, who has been our good friend since. And not until 2017, we were in a ballroom filled with 500 other Amerasians like us, children from both Black and White American fathers who served during the Vietnam War.

As we suffered discrimination from kids and adults alike, being ostracized by school officials and teachers, my mother was stressed out by all of it and finally told me it was time to stand up and defend myself. Defend, I did. I defended myself and protected my sister at all costs.

"All costs" meant violence. They threw rocks at me, and I threw back. The strategy was to be tough, so they would stop picking on us.

My mother soon realized that it was no longer safe for us to stay in Vietnam. She worried that I would get in trouble with the authorities, either from school for fighting or in the street, and end up being locked up. Life would be rough for me regardless of what I did, and when I reached the legal age, sixteen, I'd be drafted into the military to fight our neighbor, Cambodia.

In the midst of all that, thousands of Vietnamese had already fled the country by boat, and many had perished in tragic ways. Those who were caught by authorities paid a bribe so their lives would be spared or found themselves jailed and then sent to labor camps. If they had nothing to offer the corrupt authorities, their boats would be sunk out there in the ocean. My mother was aware of the risk. But something inside of her felt that it was in God's hands, so she handed my sister and me over to God. He took over from that point.

The moment I saw the figure of Jesus on the cross in that church with my friends, I believed in miracles from God, His works on and in me, and His plans for my life. That day, the seed was planted with the desire to inquire, seek, learn, believe, and follow.

Although I had two attempts of escaping Vietnam, both of those attempts failed, and I returned home safely. That would be my first miracle. It could have not ended safely. I could have been caught, and I wouldn't be writing this today.

During the third attempt, I took my little sister Linh, who was only ten years old. Both Mother and I explained to her, "We'll not be coming back." She nodded that she understood. If Linh didn't come with me, I wouldn't be writing this today. Around that age, the purpose God had given her was to be by my side, my support, my calm, my companion, my best friend, and my rock until now.

I can't imagine life without Linh. I just can't. God protected her on a couple of occasions, where we almost lost her by illness and kidnapping. She was kept safe to be my earthly angel. She helped keep us alive while we were out at sea. She gave me a reason and purpose to protect her and keep my promise to our mother.

Our next miracle was surviving the seas. The first night out, our boat faced a strong storm, which knocked the captain of the boat and all of the food that was tied to the back of it into the sea. We drifted for ten days without food and fresh water. Our boat encountered several storms during those deadly ten days.

We were the two youngest kids whose lives were spared while twenty-seven children died from starvation and dehydration. During those dark and stormy nights, I saw nothing but darkness and water. Waves after waves poured into our boat. I prayed to God for the first time. I was not chanting the chants my mother taught me. I prayed. Except I didn't know that I was praying. I was talking to God.

I remember it as if it were yesterday when I looked up in the sky and talked with Him. I pleaded for our lives, and I made a promise. I said, "God, I know You're up there looking down and seeing this. I'm begging You to make this storm stop. Please spare our lives. If I live and get to land and go where I need to go, I will find out who Jesus is."

I wholeheartedly believe God listened that night and held my promise. Pirates got onto our boat twice during those days, and we were spared from being raped. They only took our belongings, knowing that they could easily take any of us and we may never see each other again.

I had several conversations about God in refugee camps with other kids and some older than I was. There was a mix of both Catholic and Buddhist minors in the camps. I did not walk away with solid information to satisfy my inquiries. The pursuit to know Jesus remained in me for years. I'd get busy with school, jobs, and extracurricular activities, but God never left my mind. I was distracted, but He always had a way of reminding me.

We were blessed to have been placed in a loving foster home that fit and met our needs. Our foster parents remain our parents today after the foster period ended. We needed a home with parents to guide us with our new lives in America and love us like their own. We went as a family every Sunday to their Catholic church during my high school years.

Once I went to college in another city, going to church was not at the top of my list. I was away from home. I had no idea which church to attend. I thought I could go when I was home and just focus on school. My thoughts returned to Jesus often. Although, I believe God reminded me of my promise by prompting one of my college friends to invite me to church with her. Except this time, it was a Protestant church.

The pastor opened the Bible up front on the podium and gave his sermon. I hung onto every word because he said that the Bible was the Word of God. That was also the beginning of when God grabbed my attention. The Bible was a book, and I liked books; no brainer there. I would read His book, eventually. It was just a matter of when.

As I approached graduation, I thought about jobs, making money, buying a home, and sponsoring my mother over so we could reunite our family; a promise I had made with my mother when I said goodbye to her at age thirteen. I also started to think about someday having a family of my own. And if so, how would I raise my children?

Once again, God entered my mind, and I remembered that day when I was in that church in Vietnam with my friend, wanting to know who Jesus was, who God was, and not getting the answers I needed. I started to talk with God again more often. I wanted to give my children a foundation of knowing God because I did not have that as a child.

The desire to learn about God intensified. Although my ex-husband and I have gone our separate ways for twelve years now, it was with him that I had many early conversations about God. He grew up going to Sunday school. During our dating days, we talked about God often because I had a lot of questions, and he was my guide. He put it in simple terms that I could understand, especially when I asked about the Trinity. I decided this was the same God I'd been thinking about since I was a kid.

I was determined to know more about God and study. I wanted to do right by God and start my adult life right with God's blessings. As soon as I was engaged, I purchased a Bible for myself and joined Seeker's Group to study the Bible. I remember reading the Bible for the first time and being confused and scared. Fortunately, I had a patient Bible study leader who took his time explaining things to me.

In October 1994, I accepted Christ, and that was the beginning of my walk with God. I married at a church in 1995. I was baptized in 1997 on the same day my oldest daughter was dedicated.

Life can get very busy, and we sometimes forget to put God first. We get wrapped up into busyness to the point where we think we're doing it all and don't need God. But He says otherwise, and in my case, God has always gently reminded me of who He is and how He's worked in my life.

If someone were to tell me back then that I would someday raise my kids in church, serve in AWANA, be on five different church committees at one point, and then on the deaconess board, I'd say that would not be possible or felt I was not qualified to serve in that capacity. But that's what is amazing about the Lord. He guides, shapes, and prepares us to grow and be fruitful. He equips us and gives us the purpose to grow and serve in ways we least expect.

He also disciplines when we stray from His teaching. For me, pride has been disciplined, although I may not say it out loud how proud I am for "making it" or for accomplishing even small victories. Silent and quiet pride may not make itself known or broadcasted to others, but they are known and seen by God, and He ensures that we are to be humble and walk with humility. My strengths and resilience can be from days of surviving bullying or refugee camps, but I can be mistaken, thinking that they were my own strengths.

I learned what it means to pray. Although my first conversation with God was at the age of thirteen on that boat in the middle of the storms, I was mistaken that praying was only asking for something. I had periods in my younger days where I felt I was annoying God by asking for things. So, I played it tough by showing God that I didn't need to ask for anything and relied on my own. Prayerful life is not about asking for things or to be rescued from a crisis. I learned what it truly means to have loving and intimate conversations with God when I needed comfort or when I didn't trust my own decisions or choices and needed godly counsel from my heavenly Father.

"Thy rod and thy staff, they comfort me" (Ps. 23:4).

God reminds me that He's been there all along. He had carried me through those dark days. Life-changing events gave me moments where I felt defeated or life was not fair. God has grabbed me by the hand as a loving father would, showed me what plan He has for me, and I am to lean on Him for counsel and guidance in times of need.

Linh and I had a beautiful boutique between 2000–2003. I didn't join until 2001 when I moved back to town. We had customers who enjoyed our store. Linh was a natural with merchandising, knowing what to bring in to sell, and how to decorate the store with charm. My skills were behind the scenes in handling procurement, books, and numbers. My fun was producing a few clothing items I designed and sold in our store.

Another life event led us to make the decision to close the store and not sign a lease for five years. I was preparing and ready to move to California. My ex-husband had a potential lead that his employment would relocate us, and I was trying to be a good wife by being ready. The company went under, and there was no transfer. He lost his job and, in a way, I lost the store. I was heartbroken and honestly didn't think God was being fair to me. But God was talking with me in a way I was not prepared to hear. He soon perked my ears up for a Bible group study, *Purpose Driven Life*, by Rick Warren. That study was one of many that became a turning point for me. By the time I completed this study, I was at peace. I learned to be content. Several lessons were the outcomes of this study.

"I shall not want. He restoreth my soul" (Ps. 23:1b, 3a).

We were separated from our biological mother for eighteen years. I left Vietnam when I was thirteen years old and reunited with her when I was thirty-one years old. We were not prepared for the culture shock. There was no guidebook on how to navigate through these initial rough days learning each other's way. It was difficult for both mother and her daughters, but the blessings were from our former foster parents (adoptive parents) who embraced and welcomed our mother as an addition to the family. That was a blessing.

Our mother was born into a very poor family, where she suffered so much adversity, trauma, and brutality. Her resilience helped her persevere. Once she got herself out of poverty, she turned around, forgave her family, and supported them, one by one. She illustrated what it means to be loyal to the family. Her faith in Buddhism might teach different lessons of what it means to be a human and how to serve others than the Christian faith, but I believe, all in all, her good deeds onto others or her blessings onto others God has blessed by keeping her alive so she could reunite with her children.

Robbers broke into her house while she was still in Vietnam. They robbed her, stabbed her, and left her to die in the bathroom. By the miracle of God, she survived that attack and attempted murder. She was able to crawl out to the front door and scream for help. God was not done with her, and in 1999, Linh and I sponsored her to come to America. She's been blessed to enjoy the new life with her daughters and her seven grandchildren.

"Thou preparest a table before me in the presence of mine enemies" (Ps. 23:5a).

A perfect gift for perfect timing; escaping Communism for freedom and a new life was one of the reasons. The other reason was to find our fathers. We were told by our mother that we had two different fathers that were assumingly still alive around the time we left Vietnam. It never occurred to us then, or the thought did not enter our minds that they could have lost their lives in one of the battles. We assumed they were alive and well.

When we reached America, we searched for them. As a new minor and teen immigrant in America, I started to write to the military departments, but because I lacked critical information, such as full names and the correct branch, anything that would provide us any leads, I kept hitting roadblocks. Nothing was correct or available to me. We did not know whom to turn to help us with that quest.

Of course, we went on with our lives, assimilated, and grew up in America with loving foster parents, but the thought of our identity lingered. We wanted to know who we were regarding our roots and heritage, which never left our minds. Not knowing where to begin was the obstacle until Ancestry DNA was a thing that changed many lives. We also embarked on that journey of searching and to be prepared for whatever God has in store for us. I was reluctant because of the unknown and didn't want to complicate the lives of others if and when I made myself known if my father was still living and might have a family. I was worried if I would be accepted and if he would remember my mother.

I believe I was at peace once I accepted myself for my circumstances and acknowledged that God was in control of it all. It was not a random act of abandonment that I felt as a child and teen. I became reacquainted with one of my former social workers, who reminded me of Jeremiah 1:15, which I meditated on and received peace. I came to realize that I'm God's child first before I'm a child of an earthly father. I no longer felt that I was "unwanted" or abandoned by my earthly father.

"I knew you before I formed you in your mother's womb. Before you were born I set you apart and appointed you as my prophets to the nations" (Jer. 1:15 NIV).

Linh nudged me to do the DNA test as she did. My bio-father was located within a week, and I had my first conversation with him on February 7, 2018, just four days shy of my fiftieth birthday. What a gift it was. When my heart was ready to receive the gift, God revealed the gift in His timing.

"Thou anointest my head with oil, my cup runneth over" (Ps. 23:5b).

The recent miracle God blessed me with was my recent health scare with the heart. In June 2019, I had started my graduate study, a goal that I had set for myself over twenty years ago. I started the School of Social Work program in May 2019. By the second week of May, I was in the ER and returned to the ER in June with heart failure. My heart condition was grim. Yet, one year later, it is back to almost "normal." It is not short of a miracle that the heart was in that grim condition to bounce back in a short amount of time where others take years or see no improvement at all. My son was home that night to call 911. The doctor working that night in the ER, I believe, was placed there to help save me. Having the right doctor who asked the appropriate questions to correctly prescribe the correct tests for further diagnoses is so important.

"Even though I walk through the valley of the shadow of death" (Ps. 23:4a).

I remember reading and studying Psalm 23 for the first time in December 1994; the words resonated with me. It condensed and simplified for me what it means to know and have a relationship with God. It reveals who I was and who I am today in Christ. My hope, with God's guidance and teaching, I've been sharing the lessons with my children. That they, too, will learn to keep the Lord in their hearts and lean on Him.

The Lord is my shepherd;

I shall not want.

He makes me to lie down in green pastures.

He leadeth me beside still waters.

He restoreth my soul.

He leads me in paths of righteousness for His Name's sake

Even though I walk through the valley of the shadow of death.

I will fear no evil, for thou art with me; thy rod and thy staff, they comfort me.

Thou preparest a table before me in the presence of mine enemies.

Thou anointest my head with oil, my cup runneth over.

Surely goodness and mercy shall follow me all the days of my life.

And I will dwell in the house of the Lord forever (Ps. 23:1–6).

In Christ,

Minh Aimon

Gerald Anderson

As told by his daughter: Sharon Anderson Aspinwall

Sharon Anderson Aspinwall

Gerald Hugh Anderson was the third child born to Beatrice and Palmer Anderson. He had four children: three boys and a girl. He was a talented singer, entertainer, and pianist.

My daddy, Gerald Hugh Anderson, was Grandma Bea's third child and second son of Palmer Hugh Anderson. My daddy lived life to its fullest like there was no tomorrow.

Haven, Gerald, and Helen

Both of my parents were raised by Christian parents. We all went to church. Everything changed when Mom and Daddy divorced. We didn't have everything we wanted, but we always had what we needed.

Daddy loved to party and entertain; he was very talented and enjoyed singing. He learned to sing as a child in the home of Reverend Joel Norris, who married his mother, Beatrice Cobb Anderson, after his biological father, Palmer Hugh Anderson, died when my daddy was nine months old. He and his other two siblings, Haven Parker Anderson Sr. and Helen Anderson Johnson, were left without a daddy until Joel Norris married my Grandma Bea.

He was taught the Bible and grew up in a home where Christian values were both taught and lived. He always knew what was right and wrong according to the Bible. Growing up singing in church encouraged him to use his talent, which he did until just before he died.

In life, he always told us to love each other, keep our **faith**, and hold our heads high. I miss him and know for sure that he is with God.

"But as many as received Him, to them gave He power to become the sons of God, even to them that believe on His name" (John 1:12).

Legacy and Blessing

Daddy helped raise my older brother, Jerry, and three children from my mother, Greg, Sharon, and Randy. He has five grandchildren, eight great-grandchildren, and two more on the way as I write this story.

The Gerald Anderson Family

Memories are very important, and a few of them I remember vividly:

o 1960–1963: Daddy met my mother, Barbara, while she was walking down the street.

- o 1963–64: Daddy won third place in an all-night gospel singing contest when he took my mother to Waycross, Georgia, for the contest.

- o 1970: Daddy took us to church, and Daddy sang. All of us were baptized in water.

"He that believeth and is baptized shall be saved; and he that believed not shall be damned" **(Mark 16:16).**

- o 1971–1972: Dad drove us all to Naples, Florida, for Christmas. We stayed in an RV next to my Grandma Bea's home; we didn't care …we had our family, and that meant a lot to us!

- o 1972: Daddy took us on a vacation. Stop 1: Sea World in Orlando, Florida. Stop 2: back home. When we arrived in the parking lot, Dad said, **"Nope! There are too many people!"** It was a very **quiet** trip back to Jesup, Georgia!

  - o Daddy wanted to have my son Christopher go home with him to Jacksonville, Florida, for a short stay. Christopher had never been away from home before. I allowed him to go. Daddy had a singing engagement, and Christopher was to sit with my dad's friend. During the break, Christopher needed to go to the bathroom. Daddy told him to go and come right back. When Christopher failed to return immediately, Daddy became concerned and went to the bathroom; there was no Christopher! The restaurant was shut down while everyone searched for my four-year-old son. Daddy went back to the bathroom to check one more time when Christopher jumped out at him. He made Daddy so incredibly nervous and angry that he brought Christopher back to me the next day; no more stayovers with Granddaddy.

Kate, Maverick, and Christopher McReady

o   1992–1995: Daddy started a business building boat docks on the marshes of Savannah. My two brothers, Greg and Randy, who were now older, worked with him. People who knew my daddy knew he could be rather difficult to work with, especially as a boss. Daddy had a temper, and that created a need for one of them to quit. I think all of us have his temper.

o   2003: Dad encountered the loss of his friend, Shirley. I drove each weekend to Jacksonville to visit, comfort, and just be with him. He took me on a vacation to Las Vegas and Texas. We enjoyed the time together and had a great time.

o   2007: Daddy moved back to Georgia; we were excited to have him close to us because we knew we could see him often.

o   2013: The sad news came that Daddy had stage four lung cancer. He started chemo but became weaker and weaker.

o He decided he would like to go to Tennessee one last time. While he was there, he began to have seizures. Aunt Gloria and Uncle Stan went with us to Gatlinburg to be with Daddy. He eventually was allowed to travel back home.

o 2014: Daddy visited with one of his Christian friends and made everything right with God. He said he was at peace, became very humble, and demonstrated a change. That was the best blessing ever for our family.

"And they said, Believe on the Lord Jesus Christ, and thou shalt be saved, and thy house" (**Acts 16:31**).

"We will not hide them from our children, showing to the generations to come the praises of the Lord, and his strength, and his wonderful works that He has done" (**Ps. 78:4**).

o We lost him on January 8, 2014. We are blessed to know that he made everything right before he died, and we have the assurance that he is with God.

Gerald will always be remembered for his love of singing, sense of humor, and ability to communicate with people. He was blessed and knew his talents were cultivated and came from opportunities instilled in him at home and in church by blessed parents.

The Johnson Family

Helen Anderson Johnson

*H*elen Patricia Anderson Johnson was born to Palmer and Beatrice Anderson. She has been in education for fifty-five years. She has worked as a teacher, assistant principal (Tennessee), principal, (Texas), and facilitator at the graduate level. She holds certification in grades K-12. She is married to Brian Johnson. They live in Cleveland, Tennessee. They have one son, Eric, and two grandsons.

Helen Anderson Johnson

It is my desire to show our children and grandchildren that **faith** in a holy God and His Son, Jesus Christ, is the foundation that our parents and grandparents lived before us. That foundation serves as a road map for us to follow. I thank God for the godly heritage I have. "We must be devoted and committed to growing and nurturing our families through reading the Word, praying for our children, and having them involved in a church where Christ is taught. Children need to hear the great stories Jesus taught, and we need to live a life before them that shows the power the Holy Spirit gives us to live a Christian life that is an example for them to follow" (Hill 2011).

This book is in no way intended to portray a perfect family or take credit and display a haughty, prideful spirit. It is prayerfully written to inspire, demonstrate, and magnify the praiseworthy deeds and miracles in the lives of our family for our children, grandchildren, and future generations. The world today needs to know there is a living God who keeps His promises to the next generation.

"Oh, magnify the Lord with me, and let us exalt His name together" **(Ps. 34:3 NKJV).**

Growing up in a Pentecostal family allowed me to enjoy a front seat to many healings, sermons, and testimonials recounting stories of faith. My Pentecostal heritage is extremely important to my testimony and experiences. I am concerned that our young people in churches today are not hearing praiseworthy deeds of their parents and grandparents. Many are lacking the experience and knowledge of the powerful moves of God that our parents experienced and shared with us. Many young people do not know they are left with an incredible legacy and wonderful inheritance! I am concerned that many young people have never witnessed healings and powerful moves of God. Revivals in our churches and homes are needed because our children and grandchildren are vulnerable to the devices and allurement displayed in the world of technology and social media.

There is a shield of protection for them spoken of in Ephesians 6:16, *"Above all taking the shield of faith, wherewith ye shall be able to quench the fiery darts of the wicked."*

We are admonished in 1 Peter 5:8, *"Be sober, be vigilant: because your adversary, the devil, as a roaring lion, walketh about, seeking whom he may devour."*

What a description of the enemy our young people are facing! **We must tell them!** If we don't, how will they know?

God's Word will guide them in all **truth**. With the shield of faith and sword of the Spirit, we are preparing our children to face the lions in the classroom, on the playground, and in the halls of liberal colleges and universities. When they know Jesus as their Lord and Savior and understand the work of the Holy Spirit, we build a solid and secure foundation based on God's Word. We cannot be passive. We must aggressively, prayerfully, and intentionally **tell our children and grandchildren the**

praiseworthy deeds of a loving father, whose only begotten Son died for our sins.

We Are Marked for God's Commanded Blessing, a book written by Morris Cerullo, makes it very clear that there is a blessing over the children of those whose parents and grandparents trusts God and faithfully plant the seeds of the Word in their hearts at an early age. We are commanded to pass these testimonials onto our children and grandchildren and those not yet born.

Brian and Helen Johnson

"We will not hide them from their children, shewing to the generations to come the praises of the Lord, and His strength, and His wonderful works that he hath done. For He established a testimony in Jacob, and appointed a law in Israel, which he commanded our father, that they should make them known to their children: That the generation to come might know them, even the children not yet born: who should arise and declare them to their children: That they might set their hope in God, and not forget the works of God, but keep his commandments" (Ps. 78:4–6).

Where would many of us be without the prayers and teachings of our parents, grandparents, and great-grandparents? Their mission was to instill training in the **Word** inside us when we were out of the possibility for them to protect and defend us ...but never out of the presence of the Holy Spirit. They prepared us to live in a world that knows evil and lives by a standard that is the enemy to our faith.

"Where can I go from Your Spirit? Or where can I flee from Your presence? If I ascend into heaven, You are there; If I make my bed in hell, behold, You are there" (**Ps. 139:7–8**).

"In the future, when your son asks you, "What is the meaning of the stipulations, decrees and laws the Lord our God has commanded you?" Tell him: "We were slaves of Pharaoh in Egypt, but the Lord delivered us out of Egypt with a mighty hand" (**Deut. 6:20–21**).

"When our children come to us and ask about our salvation, we should tell them our faith story. We should relate what God has done in our lives and how He has delivered us." *We Will Tell: Family Devotional Guide, Day 1*

In his book, *The Place of Help*, Oswald Chamber said: "Keep recounting the wonders God has done for you."

As a former educator, I understand the importance of training up children.

Dr. Bill Bennett, former secretary of education, wrote in his book, *The Educated Child*: "Teach children in elementary school to love their country." He continued with these words: "**As soon as a child opens his lips, he should rehearse the history of his own country; he should lisp the praise of liberty, and those illustrious heroes and statesmen who have wrought a revolution in her favor**" (Bennett 1999, emphasis mine).

"Teaching patriotism in some schools is viewed as something quaint and even embarrassing; it is often viewed with suspicion as if it were brainwashing or indoctrination. His profound statements in his book are in stark contrast to what we hear from some government officials, as well as in some schools today." He concludes with the following: "**Young**

children should leave their schools loving their country more than when they entered school!" (Bennett 1999, emphasis mine).

We must pray for our parents, teachers, principals, and board members to have the boldness and commitment to stand up for our children and turn our educational systems throughout our country back to the purpose of educating children according to God's principles and the mandate of our founding fathers. I strongly believe if we raise the bar of excellence, students will adjust and rise to the occasion!

We must be intentional and deliberate in sharing our faith stories if our children learn of the miracles and blessings God has done in our homes and churches.

"We will not hide them from their descendants: we will tell the next generation the praiseworthy deeds of the Lord" (**Ps. 78:4**).

"I will open my mouth in a parable: I will utter dark sayings of old: which we have heard and known, and our fathers have told us. We will not hide them from their children, showing to generations to come the praises of the Lord, and His strength, and His wonderful works that He hath done" (**Ps. 77:11–12**).

Brian Johnson

Brian Johnson, born to Edward Bruner Johnson and Frances Marjorie Worth Johnson, has three siblings, Brenda Dixon (deceased), Bobby Joe (deceased), and Marlene Townsend. Brian lives in Cleveland, Tennessee, with his wife, Helen. They have one son, Eric, who is a critical care paramedic.

Brian Johnson – Singer and Recording Artist

Healed By The Power Of God

Brian and Brenda (Twins)

On August 13, 1940, my mother and father welcomed into their home a set of twins, Brian and Brenda. Their oldest son Bobby Joe had already died at age two, making Marlene the oldest of the three remaining children. We were born in the town of Pahokee, located on the edge of Lake Okeechobee in south central Florida. The town is a farming town with sugarcane as the primary crop. Several times a year, workers burned the cane fields to eradicate the excess leaves, which allowed the workers access to the fields. Once the cane was stacked, it was loaded onto rail cars and transported to the sugarcane refineries. We could see the cane refineries from the highway with large smokestacks.

We regularly attended the Nazarene Church on Sundays and Wednesdays. When I was four years old, I remember kneeling at an altar during vacation Bible school and asking Christ into my heart. I felt so clean inside; I wanted to tell everyone what had happened to me. My dad didn't go to church with us, but I couldn't wait to tell him that I had accepted Christ into my heart. He just said, "Okay," and went about his way.

When I entered the fourth grade in Pahokee, I began to have terrible pains in my stomach. My mother took me to the doctor; but he found nothing wrong. This continued for several months, causing me to miss many days of school. Needless to say, I failed fourth grade.

Frances Johnson – Mother of Marlene, Brenda, and Brian Johnson

My mother took me to a specialist in West Palm Beach. He determined I had a severely ulcerated stomach. I was placed on a very strict diet, consisting of bread with no crust, broiled meat, and a glass of milk with two raw eggs in it. I could eat any kind of baby food that would not irritate my stomach. My diet was so restrictive my mother would pick me up at lunchtime and take me home to eat. My weight decreased to an incredible sixty-seven pounds; I looked like skin and bones. This diet continued for several months.

One day, my mother's friend told her that Oral Roberts was coming to the Miami area. He held healing services in a 10,000-seat tent. She invited my mother to go with her to one of the services. Mother agreed, and we traveled in a stake-bodied truck with a canvas top. The trip was about one hundred miles from our home. Mother and her friend rode in the front while Brenda, Marlene, and I sat in the back. At that time, Marlene was twelve years old, and Brenda and I were ten years old. After traveling a few miles, I started feeling hungry, watching my sisters eat crackers. On the restricted diet, there was nothing for me to eat.

Once the service started, it was exciting to hear 10,000 people singing and worshiping God. Oral Roberts came to the microphone and preached a faith sermon, telling us that the Lord is our healer and all power and authority is given to Him. In his sermon, he reminded us of the many miracles Jesus performed amongst the people, and it was His will for us to be healed.

"But he was wounded for our transgressions, He was bruised for our iniquities; the chastisement of our peace was upon him; and with his stripes we are healed" (Isa. 53:5).

After he preached a powerful sermon on faith, he began praying for the sick. There were hundreds of people in the line, and I was about three-quarters of the way down the line. As we inched forward, I wondered if he would pray for me before the closing of the healing line. I remember walking up the long ramp and standing before him. He looked at my healing card, which had been filled out prior to getting in the line, and said, "Okay, another Nazarene."

He laid his hand on my head, and I felt something like electricity surge through my body. I told my mother how I felt when he laid his hand on me, and she replied, "You're healed!"

We headed home after the service when I suddenly realized I was still very hungry. I saw that same box of Ritz crackers sitting in the back of the truck by one of my sisters. I told her I wanted some crackers. I heard her say, "You're not supposed to eat crackers." She knew the roughage of the crackers would irritate the ulcers within my stomach. I ate every cracker left in the box on the way home, and thankfully, never had pain.**I was healed by the power of Almighty God!**

The next morning was Sunday. I got up and went into the kitchen, where Daddy was cooking breakfast. He asked, "What do you want to eat, son?"

I asked what he was cooking, and he responded that he was cooking some greasy sausage. To his surprise, I told him I would also have some greasy sausage. I enjoyed eating "real" food for the first time in many months, and never had a reaction to the grease. To this day, I have no problems with my stomach. I am now in my 80s—no ulcers, and I know it was God who healed me.

Pahokee was located near the lake; the ground consisted of muck, which was moist, soggy, and black. Everyone had a vegetable garden.

My dad worked in a body shop repairing wrecked automobiles. To everyone in the community, he was known as Dick. He would repair and restore the vehicles, making them look as good as new. Because of his excellent work and strong work ethics, he had many clients in the area. He was always a good provider for our family. His business grew, and he decided to become an independent business owner. He and a new partner, Bob, bought a piece of land and built a small shop. Bob was the mechanic, and Daddy was the body man. They worked in this partnership for several years. One day, Daddy decided to sell out his portion of the partnership, and we moved to Naples, Florida.

For many years, my grandmother lived in Naples, located on the Gulf Coast, forty miles south of Fort Myers. During that time, Naples was a small, quaint little town of about 1,500 people and had one school. Fishermen would catch the fish, ice them down, and ship the fish to other areas of the country by rail car. Fishing generated the primary income of the community as Naples had a fishing pier that extended into the gulf 1,000 feet.

At one time, the pier was touted as the longest pier in the country. Grandma loved to fish at the pier and would frequent it often. There was a concession stand midway out on the pier where one could buy snacks and drinks. Prior to moving to Naples, our family vacationed there during the summer. In the evenings, the people would gather to watch the beautiful sunsets and enjoy the cool breezes while getting relief from the summer heat since no one had air conditioning. It became the daily social gathering place of the community.

The pier propelled me into my singing career. My grandmother, being a businesswoman, and never letting an opportunity pass, took advantage of the gatherings on the pier. She would call Marlene, Brenda, and me to come near her, and she would tell the audience, "These are my grandkids, and they are going to sing for you."

After we would finish singing, she would take off her big straw hat, which she always wore when she fished, turn it upside down, and take an offering "for the grandkids." However, we never saw the offering.

On the other side of the pier is where you could sell your catch of the day. Many times, Grandma would be at the pier before daylight, catching fish and selling them. She sometimes would stay on the pier well into the night, only to repeat that action the next day.

The Johnson Family

When we moved to Naples, I started fourth grade in school. Church was a vital part of our lives in Pahokee. We started attending Church of God with my grandmother. It was a small Pentecostal church just off

10th Street. We became involved in the church, and later on, received the infilling of the Holy Spirit.

The pastor of the church, Reverend John Allen, heard about my healing and asked me to share my story with the congregation, which I did. It was during a time when Christianity was respected in the public school system. Often times, the school principal invited a minister from the community to be a guest speaker at the school assembly. He invited our pastor, John Allen, to be a guest speaker.

Pastor Allen mentioned that I had been healed of an ulcerated stomach. He called me up to give my testimony to the student body. The students sat there with great attention and listened intently to my testimony. After that day, when we were on the playground and students were playing, if one said a slang word in my presence, he would apologize for talking like that in front of me. I appreciated their respect for my faith. This continued throughout my high school years.

"Bless the Lord, oh my soul: and all that is within me, bless His holy name. Bless the Lord, oh my soul, and forget not all his benefits; who forgiveth all thine iniquity; who healeth all thy diseases" (Ps. 103:1–3).

After high school, I enrolled in Lee College, located in Cleveland, Tennessee. I became involved in several musical groups. God allowed me to fulfill my dream of serving Him when I auditioned and was selected to sing in the Lee College Touring Choir (now known as the Lee Singers). The choir traveled to many states, singing in both large and small churches. It was during chapel at Lee that I experienced a strong spiritual foundation in classes with godly professors.

Dick, Marlene, and Kevin Townsend

I always enjoyed singing in church with my two sisters, Marlene and Brenda. We all attended Lee together and periodically sang for chapel services and other events. Brenda was a gifted musician, and she accompanied me at weddings, camp meetings, and in the local church. She played skillfully, both organ and piano, and taught piano lessons. Brenda was gifted in writing music as well. She initially took piano lessons from Dr. Delton Alford, whose dad pastored the Naples Church of God.

One of Brenda's greatest accomplishments is teaching piano to her nephew, Kevin Townsend. Kevin is the son of our sister Marlene and her husband, Dick Townsend. Kevin serves as pianist in a large church in Lakeland, Florida. He is a protégé of Brenda. He said he accepted Christ in vacation Bible school.

> I credit my parents for living a consistent life before me. Going to church, thinking, and talking about God daily was the normal conversation in our home. I started taking piano lessons in Naples with my aunt, Brenda. Even though I had other piano teachers in my

life, along with teaching scales theory and technique, she added an extra element, learning to play church music. In fifth grade, she encouraged me to play in church. She was a strong influence in my choosing church music. I hold a degree in music from Palm Beach Atlantic University.

Kevin Townsend, told via phone call to Helen Johnson, August 2021.

Brenda died on March 15, 2019, much too early; I miss her very much. She left two daughters, Jennifer Dixon, who worked in Faith Ministries and is an educator, and Kimberly Dostal, who is married to Russell Dostal and has one grandson, Tucker. God raised Kimberly after having brain surgery for a brain tumor; she works part-time and now can drive. She is a testimony of faith and healing. Brenda was married to Lee Dixon, whom she met while attending Lee College. She was dedicated to her music ministry to the very end, and her legacy lives on!

"I will sing of the mercies of the Lord forever: with my mouth will I make known thy faithfulness to all generations" (**Ps. 89:1**).

Eric Johnson

Eric is the son of Brian and Helen Johnson. He is married to Erica, and they have two sons, Brandon and Tyler. He currently works for Bradley County Emergency Services in Cleveland, Tennessee, as a certified paramedic with critical care designation.

Eric Brian Johnson

"That I may publish with the voice of thanksgiving, and tell of thy wondrous works" (**Ps. 26:7**).

In summer 1979, having just completed the fifth grade and having played basketball on the Naples Christian Academy Crusaders basketball team, I, along with several of the players on our team, attended summer basketball camp at the University of Tennessee in Knoxville. I traveled with a friend and his parents and enjoyed the beautiful UT

130

campus. I felt privileged to attend the camp and work with coaches from Tennessee.

After a week of intensive training, my parents and I left for vacation to Washington DC. My cousin Rick Norris traveled with us. My grandmother was a nurse and worked in Washington. Rick and I enjoyed the sights and memorials in Washington and military concerts that were held on the Capitol steps. We would meet our grandmother each evening for dinner, and that was a treat.

Excited is not the word to describe my feelings, as I anticipated the basketball season for the next school year. Normally during the summer, my friends and I spent most of our time at the beach. It was during that year I received my certification as a scuba diver. Anything involved in water sports, such as snorkeling and water skiing, we did it!

My paternal grandfather lived in Lakeland, Florida, which is about 160 miles from Naples. We would often visit on the weekends, and he would send me home with vegetables from his garden. Our neighbors around the lake became my customers; I would sell the vegetables to them for money to buy tennis shoes, which I loved, school supplies, and clothes.

One beautiful sunny afternoon, I took my eight-foot Styrofoam sailboat onto the lake to deliver the vegetables from my grandfather's garden with Clementine, my basset hound, as my first mate. What a job, sailing and making money at the same time—no overhead!

We had no concerns of any kind, knowing there was a four-foot alligator living in the lake, which often swam alongside of us. We just made sure neither of us fell out of the boat. With deliveries made and cash collected, we headed home with no worries of the alligator because I was the pilot of the ship, and Clementine was my first mate.

It was monsoon season in Naples, and the clouds began to roll in with loud claps of thunder. My mother summoned me to come home because of the approaching storm.

I pulled the boat to shore and secured it; the winds began to gust, causing me to bump my knee. Clementine followed right behind me.

For once, she obeyed my orders not to chase the ducks around the lake. Suddenly, a very large soft knot appeared on my leg.

My mother contacted our family doctor for an appointment. He examined my knee and sent me to a well-known orthopedic surgeon. This was devastating to a sixth-grader who loved sports and was especially interested in playing basketball. When the surgeon reviewed my MRI, he told my parents there was a very large tumor in my leg, and surgery was a necessity. He indicated that he would not know for sure until he performed the surgery whether the tumor was in the growth plate. If so, I could have a limp for the rest of my life, or a worst-case scenario, if it was malignant, the leg might have to be removed.

"Though I walk in the midst of trouble, you will revive me, and your right hand will save me" **(Ps. 123:7).**

Before the surgery, my local church, Naples Church of God, the pastor, Reverend Walter Lauster, with my teachers and friends from Naples Christian Academy, prayed for me. With school starting in a few days and a long recovery ahead of me and therapy to follow, I felt as though my basketball career was over.

I accepted Christ at an early age and was baptized soon after. I grew up in a home where prayer was very important. My parents and I had prayer and family devotions every morning before I went to school, but at this time, for a twelve-year-old, all I could think about was the nightmare I was facing.

The morning of the surgery, the doctor came in to reassure my parents and grandparents that he was sure the surgery would go well and I would be fine; however, his major concern was still the size of the tumor. He reiterated what he had said in his office earlier, that my leg could be shorter than the other, and if the tumor was malignant, my worst-case scenario would be the loss of the leg. The surgery went well, and God answered our prayers. Because of the size of the tumor, six inches long and two inches wide, it was sent to Johns Hopkins Hospital in Baltimore to be used as a teaching tool in the hospital.

"One generation shall praise thy works to another, and shall declare thy mighty acts" **(Ps. 145:4).**

After going through eight weeks of therapy, having to be homeschooled, no participation in sports, and missing a semester of school, I still had Clementine, my first mate and constant companion. I know that God heals. I am blessed, and every day I'm reminded of His blessing when I look at the large scar.

We have declared that we will tell!

Erica and Eric Johnson – Parents of Brandon and Tyler Johnson

Brandon and Amanda Johnson with Harlee and Harper

Brian "Tyler" Johnson

Tyler Johnson is the son of Eric and Erica Johnson. He currently works at Bradley County Emergency Medical Services as a paramedic. Additionally, he is a deputy medical examiner for Bradley County, Tennessee. He is the director of emergency services for the City of Etowah, Tennessee, where he lives.

Brian Tyler Johnson – Paramedic and Deputy Medical Examiner

I often rode my mountain bike with my brother Brandon several times a week, and this particular week was no different. Visions, dreams, and goals were always important to me. I played football in middle school and all four years of high school. I received an academic scholarship to Carson Newman College to play college level football. During high school, I volunteered 400-plus hours at my hometown fire/rescue service and received recognition for this task.

It is no surprise that I would follow in the footsteps of my parents, who are both paramedics. I finished high school and enrolled in classes to obtain certification in the State of Tennessee as an emergency medical technician (EMT). I could supplement my educational expenses by working as an EMT.

I completed the course work, passed the state exam, and became a licensed emergency medical technician. My duties were rather mundane until I got experience working in the field with paramedics. I was primarily assigned as an ambulance driver, working with a paramedic in charge of the patient. Often, our call would be an emergency, but other times, it would be a non-emergency patient transport.

Brandon, Erica, Eric, and Tyler – First Responders

During my first semester at Carson Newman College, my mother was stricken with a stroke, causing her right side to become paralyzed. At the end of the first semester, I decided to transfer to a local college, Tennessee Wesleyan College, in my hometown. My scholarship was an academic scholarship, and I was allowed to transfer all my credits to TWC.

My dream job would be to work for the FBI in the narcotics division. Now that I had received my EMT certification, I was able to work part-time while attending classes in the criminal justice division.

It was a clear, crisp, fall morning on November 12, 2012, when my call came in to transport a special needs high school student to his regular therapy session at Erlanger Hospital in Chattanooga, Tennessee. The hospital is about an hour's drive from Athens, Tennessee.

Every morning, my grandmother would text me and tell me she was praying for me. That day, she texted this scripture:

"The angels of the Lord encampeth around them that fear Him and delivereth them" (**Ps. 34:7**).

All of my life, I grew up attending Sunday school and church. I learned about God's intervention in the lives of people. Never in my wildest dreams did I think of the incredible tragedy that I would encounter that morning. But God knew.

The paramedic I worked with was assigned to the special needs patient. This patient had a special needs nurse who accompanied him. She rode in the back of the ambulance with the patient, along with the paramedic. The patient knew us very well because this was a routine appointment at Erlanger Hospital for his therapy. The patient's grandmother accompanied the patient and rode in the front seat of the ambulance with me. We took a secondary route, Highway 58 South, instead of Interstate 75.

We were unaware that earlier that morning, an all-points bulletin had been sent out from the Tennessee Highway Patrol, asking law enforcement to be aware of a green pickup truck with two females in it, traveling erratically at a high rate of speed. I distinctly remember looking at the speedometer and observed we were averaging about 55 mph. I looked at my watch to make sure we were on schedule for the patient's appointment at the hospital.

Tennessee is known for its rolling hills, deep valleys, and beautiful mountains. I observed a rather steep drop-off on the right side of the highway and commented to the patient's grandmother that it must be twenty or thirty feet deep. I knew if someone ran off the road, it would be catastrophic. It was extremely steep.

I looked up and observed we were approaching a green pickup truck following closely behind an SUV. The vehicle fit the description of the all-points bulletin by the THP. Suddenly, the green pickup pulled out to pass the SUV, placing the pickup directly on a head-on collision course with our ambulance. I touched the brakes a couple of times, hoping the driver of the green pickup would fall back into her lane; however, it did not happen. I realized the inevitable ...we were going to collide. I steered the ambulance as close to the right side of my lane as I possibly could without going over the embankment, hoping to deflect, to some degree, the impact.

We hit almost head-on. The impact was so severe the engine was ripped from the frame of the ambulance and came to rest about one hundred feet from the rest of the wreck. The engine in the green pickup exploded on impact, with engine parts scattered over a large area. The ambulance was now on its side.

Fortunately, we did not go over the embankment. Thankfully, we were all wearing seatbelts. The special needs patient was buckled in and miraculously sustained only bruises but no serious injuries. The paramedic suffered a broken leg. The other two passengers received non-life-threatening injuries.

Because of the impact and we were on our side, I found myself hanging upside down, strapped in by my seatbelt. The assessment of the others lasted for forty-five minutes before they could get to me. I had to be extricated by the firemen on the scene, with only bruises on my chest from my seatbelt ...a true miracle since I was driving the ambulance and took the full force of the impact.

"One generation shall praise thy works to another, and shall declare thy mighty acts" (Ps. 145:4).

My dad was working at the Bradley County Emergency Ambulance Service that morning and heard that a wreck had occurred on Highway 58. He heard the radio transmission regarding the wreck and knew that was my assigned transport. He quickly jumped into an ambulance and raced west down Highway 60 and turned south on Highway 58 to the scene. Upon arrival, he observed that I was still strapped into my seat belt, hanging there, waiting to be extricated. I can remember his rushing over and quickly, urgently asking, "Tyler, are you okay?"

I looked at him and calmly said, "I'm okay, just hanging around."

Unfortunately, and very heartbreaking to recall, I could see a canvas covering the two young females who died upon impact. They never returned home to their small children. Earlier that morning, my grandmother sent me a biblical text, as she often did, telling me that "the angels of the Lord encamped around those that fear Him, and delivereth them." She also told me she was praying for me and to have a great day! What a miracle that day in November!

"For He shall give his angels charge over thee, to keep thee in all thy ways. They shall bear thee up in their hands, lest thou dash thy foot against a stone" (Ps. 91:11–12).

My great grandmother Johnson led me in the Sinner's Prayer at a very early age. That decision had a powerful influence on me during my teen years. The best decision of my life instilled a firm ethical foundation. The self-discipline I learned during those years established my goals and dreams for the future.

I enrolled in the second semester and planned to get a degree in criminal justice and work for the FBI. I spent the next three and a half years working toward that degree before graduating in 2014 with a degree in criminal justice and forensics. I continued working as an EMT to support my educational needs.

The job as an EMT is very stressful. The level of stress is, oftentimes, lowered by working out and having fun with co-workers. We share many stories as support to one another in our work.

After working for several years as an EMT, I enrolled in paramedic school, still wanting to work for the FBI.

On January 1, 2016, my grandmother sent a prayer request to the Daystar Christian Television Network in Dallas, Texas. It was my twenty-fourth birthday. The prayer request was that I would find direction to pursue a master's degree and grow spiritually in my walk with Christ.

"Trust in the Lord with all thine heart; and lean not unto thine own understanding. In all thy ways acknowledge him, and he will direct your path" (**Prov. 3:5**).

My grandmother quoted to me Psalm 37:5, *"**Commit thy way unto the Lord, and he shall bring it to pass.**"*

That same day, she sent me a text telling me what she had done.

On March 11, 2016, I received a text message from her. She often did this as an encouragement to me. The message said: *Tyler, there is no problem that you will experience today that God is not greater; hang in there!*

Also that day, the telephone rang at noon at my grandmother's house, and a minister from the Daystar Christian Television Network asked how I was doing. The minister said the prayer team was going over prayer requests and wanted to follow up on the request my grandmother had sent in on January 1. Again, at 5 pm that same day, my grandmother sent a text message saying she was praying for me.

At 10:00 pm, my paramedic partner and I pulled into the station to restock the ambulance before leaving our shift, ready for the third shift to take our place. It was routine to gather information and restock the ambulances for the next shift. I was in a good mood, laughing and having fun when suddenly I felt ill. I told the other members of the crew that I didn't feel well when suddenly I passed out and collapsed on the floor. My co-workers thought I was teasing, lying there on the floor, lifeless.

There were six paramedics and six EMTs present. Suddenly, they realized I had a serious problem and began CPR. They transported me to the nearest hospital. The doctors at the hospital made the assessment that I was in cardiac arrest. I was immediately transported to a large hospital in Knoxville, Tennessee.

After arriving at the hospital, the assessment was that I had five blockages in my heart and must immediately have bypass surgery.

The doctors performed the surgery; however, one artery could not be addressed due to its location and size. So, they limited their work to a quadruple bypass.

I was twenty-three years old, still thinking and dreaming I would someday be working for the FBI. I certainly was not expecting a heart attack and quadruple bypass surgery.

After surgery, I was off work for a couple of weeks before returning. I thought I could resume where I left off before surgery; however, before the day was over, I realized I was not in any condition to do the strenuous work with patients that I sometimes had to do. I took the next seven months off until I felt I was completely healed enough to go back to work.

My mom and dad had a pet dog. Roscoe was my friend throughout this ordeal. He sensed something was wrong with me, would not jump up wanting to play, but stayed right by my side during the recovery period. He would just sit by my side with his head on my lap. The very day I felt like I could go back to work, Roscoe snuggled up to me, placed his nose on my chest, sniffed the scar several times, then suddenly, he decided it was time to play again as if he knew I had recovered and was ready to return to work.

I've been back to work for several years now and can truly say that God is good! I have had no re-occurrences of heart problems, and my health is good! I do take medicine to control my cholesterol, but I am living life at its finest. I am now a certified paramedic and have enrolled in the next step, which is critical care paramedic. That schooling will begin in fall 2021. I also am currently pursuing my master's degree in criminal justice at Columbia Southern University and hope to graduate sometime in the very near future. **TO GOD BE THE GLORY!**

References

Reference used throughout entire book

We Will Tell: Family Devotional Guide,

Cleveland, TN: Westmore Church of God. Days 1, 2, 3, 4, 5.

Reference used in Beatrice Cobb

Cobb, Keith. M.D. (2010). *The Grief Survival Handbook: A Guide from Heartache to Healing*. Vancouver, British Columbia: Trafford Publishing Co.

References used in Helen Anderson Johnson

Griffith, Wanda Gore. (1994). *Sand In My Shoes*. Cleveland, TN:

Pathway Press. PP. 33, 73, 74, 91.

Bennett, William J., Chester E. Finn, Jr., John T.E. Cribb, Jr. (1999). *The Educated Child: A Parent's Guide from Preschool Through Eighth Grade*. New York: A Touchstone Book, Simon & Schuster. PP. 191, 192, 199.

Copeland, Gloria. (May, 2019). "*A Legacy of Faith*". Daystar News. Daystar.com/Gloria Copeland. P. 2.

Baker, Michael L., Ed. D. (Oct. 2019). *My Pentecostal Heritage: I Am Blessed!* The Evangel: Cleveland, TN: Church of God Publishing House, P. 21.

Cerullo, Morris. (2000). *Marked for God's Commanded Blessing.* San Diego, CA: Morris Cerullo World Evangelism. PP. 21, 25, 27, 29, 47, 50, 51.

Hill, Paula. (2011). *Heart Songs: A Devotional Journey for Women.* Cleveland, TN: Tim Hill Ministries, P. 51, 162.

Omartian, Stormie. (2009). *The Power of Praying for Your Adult Children.* Eugene, OR: Harvest House Publishers, Introduction.

Endorsements

W ith so many churches having kids' church, youth services, mid-week Bible studies, and groups (all of those are good things!), it seems as though there's a disconnect between generations in our churches. Gone are those corporate Wednesday night prayer meetings, where those younger in the faith hear of those mountains moved, victories claimed, and prayers answered in the lives of people they actually know. This book compels us to see the faithful hand of God fulfilling His promises and answering prayers through generations.

Helen Johnson has taken family history, anecdotes, and glimpses into the rural South of old and woven a tapestry of faith and the power our prayers have for future generations.

Cindy Morrow

Former English Teacher

Cleveland, Tennessee

As a parent myself, I am understanding more and more about the importance of leaving a lasting legacy for our families. I am so thankful for Helen Johnson and Dr. Julia Stanley-Mack for their willingness to write this book. *Legacy of Faith* is a treasure that is filled with beautifully written stories of God's faithfulness and love to His people. Helen and Julia share from their own personal experiences and those of their family members the fact that God wants to save and bless each of our families. When we build our foundation on His truth, generational blessings abound. This book is **amazing** and will provide encouragement and support to those who truly desire to leave a legacy of faith for their loved ones. Mrs. Johnson and Dr. Stanley-Mack have written a masterpiece, and you don't want to miss it!

Dr. Jason Robinson

Associate Professor of Education

Lee University

Cleveland, Tennessee

HELEN ANDERSON JOHNSON

Helen began her teaching career on Eleuthera Island in the Bahamas, serving as a missionary. After graduating from Lee College (1961) and Georgia Southern University (1964), her ministry began in public education, teaching English and literacy classes. Eleven of those years were served in Christian schools in both administration and classrooms. She has served in adjunct/facilitator positions for the Schools of Education for the University of Tennessee in Knoxville and Chattanooga.

Helen served as president of Hamilton County Reading Association, state president of Tennessee Reading Association, and "Distinguished Classroom Teacher" of Hamilton County. She was a Stokley fellow at the University of Tennessee, in Knoxville, where she received a master's degree in administration and supervision.

Helen Anderson Johnson

DR. JULIA NORRIS STANLEY-MACK

Julia (Julie) Beatrice Norris Stanley-Mack has pastored Life Spring Worship Center in Bloomingdale, Georgia, for thirty-seven years. She is a certified counselor with the American Association of Christian Counselors.

For the past twenty-three years, she has served as the administrator of LSCA, a state-accredited academy. She is the founder and president of the Master's College of Georgia (training for men and women in biblical studies, equipping them for ministry). She is the director of a local FM gospel radio, WSGF.

Julia Norris Stanley-Mack

CPSIA information can be obtained
at www.ICGtesting.com
Printed in the USA
BVHW012209151222
654394BV00029B/708